MW01659751

Credit Repair Made Simple

First Edition
COPYRIGHT 2000
ISBN: 0-9700607-0-X
Library of Congress Number: 190948

By
Brian Eichhorn

BEAK Press
24 Byron Drive
Richmond Hill, GA 31324
1-800-990-9981
912-691-1715
FAX 912-691-1182

ACKNOWLEDGEMENTS

This book would not have been possible if it were not for the support of several people. Thank you to Matthew Wallace. If it were not for him I would still be on page one. Thank you to Linda Salter for the long hours editing this book. Most of all I would like to thank my beautiful wife Kathy. She is without a doubt the best wife a guy could have.

All information contained within this book is for informational and educational purposes only- designed to help the reader become a more informed consumer by illustrating the value of good credit. Every effort has been made to make sure all examples, ideas, and suggestions are accurate, but there is no guarantee or warranty by the author to the accuracy or effectiveness of all information contained within. The author will not be held liable for any inconsistencies, or any consequences that may arise from the use of this book.

CONTENTS

Chapter One

Your Credit Profile

In the financial world your credit is one of the most important assets you can have. With good credit, you command the best interest rates available as well as receive respect when dealing with lenders. Having good credit allows you a more comfortable lifestyle. You will be paying less on credit cards, mortgages, car loans, etc. and more of your income will be freed for the luxuries you want in life.

While it is important to have good credit, you must also know just how good your credit is. There are many people out there who actually have good credit, but don't realize it. A loan officer, on the other hand, can easily recognize this. If this happens, you can realistically expect to be taken advantage of. Educating yourself is the key to avoiding such a situation.

When applying for a loan at the bank, one is often met with discriminating eyes. All too often we are judged by our outward appearance. But, "credit wears no clothes". The nicest dressed man with poor credit is quickly denied a loan and shown the door. The shabby dressed man, on the other hand, with perfect credit, is likely to get that loan. If you know your credit is good you should feel confident as you apply for this loan. It does not matter a person's race, creed, or religion. What matters is a person's ability to repay the loan. If they are able to do this, they will receive the respect they deserve, and most likely the loan.

Yet many people, young and old, don't realize the importance of good credit. I didn't when I was young. When I was twenty years old and without a job, I had an Amoco credit card. Until they canceled it due to lack of payment, I ate breakfast, lunch, and dinner there. Believe me, Amoco food does not make for a well-balanced diet.

I didn't have a job, so I surely didn't have the money to pay the monthly bill. But, I didn't care. I knew, eventually, I would pay them back. Simply because, it was the way I was raised. It didn't matter to me if they didn't get paid back until a year later, as long as they were eventually paid back. A friend of mine asked me if I cared that my credit would be affected by not paying the bill on time. I told him no. My rationale was, I didn't need credit. In my eyes, I didn't need good credit until I was about 27. Don't ask me how I arrived at that age. Maybe I figured that would be when I would need to buy a car or really start to make something of my life. Heck, I was in college and this wasn't a time to be worried about something that had no immediate effect on me.

As I got older I realized that credit was important. Very important. When I started in the mortgage business I met clients who had less than perfect credit. Some had down-right rotten credit. Many of them had the belief that as long as they eventually paid the loan back, they should have good credit.

I had one gentleman in particular who told me his credit was great. He told me about the loans he had received in the past and how every one was paid off. When I pulled his credit report, sure enough, every account showed up as being paid off; but not until they had been placed with a collection agency. When I inquired about his pay history on the accounts he agreed that they had indeed gone to collection. He did pay the loans off as soon as the collection agents had called him. So, in his eyes, he should have good credit.

The sad thing about that situation is he isn't the only one. I have had at least a dozen clients that had the same belief. And, I know there are many more people in this world that have the same misconceptions about what credit really is, and the importance of it.

In the following chapters, I will explain what credit bureaus are, how they work, and what they mean to you, the borrower. Armed with that understanding we will then tackle repairing your credit. The legal way.

Chapter Two

Credit Bureaus

Before we get into what credit bureaus are, you need to get a copy of your credit report from the three major credit bureaus.

You are entitled to one free copy of your credit report each year if you:

1) Have reason to believe your credit report contains inaccurate information as a result of being a victim of fraud.
2) Are unemployed and seeking employment.
3) Are receiving public welfare assistance.

You may also receive a free copy of your credit report if you have been denied credit, employment, or housing within the last 60 days.

By Federal law, if you have been denied credit, employment, or housing, the creditor who denied you must provide a reason for denial. They must tell you which credit bureau they used in making their decision. You will only be entitled to the credit report they used. Include a copy of the denial letter with your request.

If you don't meet any of the listed requirements you may have to pay a small fee. Usually $8-$10 per credit report.

You may also obtain a copy by visiting a local credit bureau. You can find one listed in your yellow pages.

To obtain a copy from one of the three major bureaus, send the following information:

Full Name (including Jr. or Sr.)
Current Address, City, State, Zip Code
All Addresses in Last Five Years
Date of Birth
Social Security Number
Home Telephone

You must include proof of address with each request (i.e. copy of drivers license, utility bill, phone bill, etc.)

You must sign your name at the end of the request.

If you have been denied credit, enclose a copy of the denial letter with your request for a copy of your credit report.

Addresses of the Major Credit Bureaus

Equifax
PO Box 740256
Atlanta, GA 30374
800-685-1111

Experian (TRW)
PO Box 2104
Allen, TX 75013-2104
800-682-7654

Trans Union
PO Box 34012
Fullerton, CA 92834
800-916-8800

There are three major credit bureaus where creditors receive information about your credit history. Equifax, Experian (formerly TRW), and Trans Union. The bureaus act as information gatherers. They store information on virtually every adult in the United States.

Credit bureaus are not government agencies. Credit bureaus are for-profit companies, which make money by selling your credit file to businesses or individuals who have a bona fide interest in your financial profile. These bureaus also sell your name to marketers who request certain demographic or financial parameters. For example, persons having more than three major credit cards in the state of Florida, or people with a total of $10,000+ in credit card balances in the United States. No specific information about the person is provided, only certain parameters. To opt out of the release of your name for marketing purposes see page 65.

Credit bureaus use a credit profile model that was developed by Fair Isaac & Co. to generate a score ranging from 375 to 900 for individuals. Credit scoring is a process designed to predict the future; whether or not you'll live up to the obligations you incur today. Many lenders base their decision on whether or not to lend to you on the credit score. The higher the better. There are many factors used in determining your credit score. The following factors are weighted the heaviest when determining your score:

1. Major derogatory items on your report
    A. bankruptcy
    B. foreclosure
    C. judgements
    D. collections
    E. slow pay on accounts
2. Time at present job
3. Time at present address
4. Ratio of balances to available credit lines (the lower the better)
5. Number of recent inquiries
6. Number of credit lines on your report
7. Years you have had credit in the credit bureau database
8. Occupation (Professionals are given more points)
9. Homeowners receive more points.
10. Age

Credit bureaus do not verify information they receive. They only gather it. It is up to consumers to question any mistakes. It is estimated that over one third of all consumers have one or more incorrect items of information in their credit reports. Sometimes these errors can effect an application for a loan or a potential job by lowering your credit score. However, there are laws that protect you if you find errors on your credit report.

The *Federal Fair Credit Reporting Act* states that when a consumer disputes any information in his/her credit file, the credit bureau must verify the accuracy of the information with the creditor who reported the information within a reasonable amount of time. The FTC is vague on the exact time allowed. Some disputes can be cleared in a short amount of time, while other complicated disputes might take months to resolve. If the credit bureau is unable to verify the information within a reasonable amount of time, or the information is not 100% correct, it must be removed. The Fair Credit Reporting Act will be your tool in correcting and improving your credit report and credit score.

Chapter Three

Factors That Influence Your Score

Major Derogatory items on Your Report

Bankruptcy

Bankruptcy, depending on when it occurred, can cause a lender to automatically deny you a loan. The reason is simple. If you had to file bankruptcy, you obviously had a problem with your finances. Your spouse may have been laid off from work, died, or had an unexpected medical emergency, which put a drain on your income. Maybe you could not manage your money properly. If you have filed multiple bankruptcies, creditors will almost certainly deny you credit. Sometimes, however, one bankruptcy can show up on your credit report as multiple bankruptcies. For example, you have added more items into a plan such as a chapter 13, or if you moved from a chapter 13 to a chapter 7. Another example is, if you had a bankruptcy dismissed rather than discharged. A creditor may look at it as if you couldn't even keep up with the bankruptcy plan you originally entered because you couldn't even pay your bills.

A bankruptcy can stay on your credit report for up to ten years. My experience has been that virtually all bankruptcies get reported to the credit bureaus once they are filed. However, I have seen many bankruptcies that do not get reported as being settled. If you pay out your bankruptcy as agreed, you will be "discharged" from your bankruptcy. Your credit report should state that you were discharged and the date of the discharge. If you did not pay out your bankruptcy as agreed, you will be "dismissed" from your bankruptcy. Your credit report should state that you were dismissed and the date of the dismissal. Lenders look more favorably towards applicants who were discharged rather than dismissed.

Foreclosure

A lender views a foreclosure as being just as bad as a bankruptcy. Sometimes even more. The reason is simple. A home is a person's most valuable asset next to their family. It provides one of the most important necessities in life, shelter. A lender reasons that a person in trouble financially will let everything else go before they will allow their house to be foreclosed on. If you couldn't even pay your house payment, do you think a lender expects you to pay on any other type of loan?

Judgements

Judgements throw up red flags because, fair or not, they reflect that someone took you to court to collect on a bill that you would not, or could not pay. Even if you are 100% right, but couldn't prove your case in court, it will show up on your credit as a judgement against you. When I was living in an apartment, my door was broken. I called maintenance to get it fixed and got hit with a bill of $230. I thought this was excessive so I refused to pay. After some negotiation with the management group we both decided to take it to small claims court. At small claims court it was reduced to $135, which I promptly paid. However, for the next seven years I had a judgement on my credit report. Even though, in a sense, I won. I wasn't disputing that I owed. I was disputing the excessive amount. The only way I could have protected my credit would have been to pay the amount in question and then sue the management group.

Judgements can stay on your credit report for up to seven years. Towards the end of the seven years, the creditor can go to the courts and file suit again to have the judgement reinstated for another seven years.

Creditors are not likely to refile against you unless they believe you have an asset that they could have the judgement attached to. After the courts render a verdict of judgement against you, a form is filed with the court. This changes the judgement to a lien against you and anything you own that is recorded at the courthouse. If you own a house, then a judgement would become a lien against your house until the time expired on the judgement. If you were to refinance or sell your house, you would then have to pay off the judgement.

Collections

The normal procedure for a seriously delinquent account would be to place it either with a collection department within the creditor's business or assign it to a collection company.

This is when you start getting annoying phone calls from the collection agents seeking payment from you. What you have to realize is that most collection agents receive a commission on money they receive from delinquent accounts. This is how they make their living, but sometimes they may get too aggressive in seeking repayment. **(See Fair Debt Collection, page 45)**

Collections are subject to interpretation by each creditor. Some creditors are more lenient when medical collections show up. Many lenders realize that when medical bills are incurred there can be a lag time with insurance companies paying their part. For instance, if you are involved in an auto accident that was someone else's fault the medical bills may be resolved through the legal system. If there are large balances on the collections or excessive medical collections this may raise a larger red flag.

There are certain collections that lenders definitely do not like to see. If you have a phone company, utility company, or cable company that you didn't pay and they put your account into collections that will look like you have a total disregard for these sometimes- necessary services. A lender may look at it, as "you couldn't even pay your light bill, what makes me think you can pay me".

Bad check collections are another red flag for the lender. A lender views these types of accounts as "You wrote checks that were bad and didn't rectify the situation. You left the merchant "high and dry". If you have several bad check collections, you will not be considered a desirable applicant.

Charge-offs

Charge-offs exhibit a disregard for paying items such as credit cards. If a credit card account goes unpaid for a long enough time and has already passed through the collection department of the creditor, the creditor may charge-off the account. Meaning they aren't expecting any payment from you and write the account off as a loss. Usually, a charge-off is against an account that has no collateral against it, such as a credit card. A lender may deny you a credit card if charge-offs show up on your credit report because of the increased liability.

Child Support

Delinquent child support payments can now be reported to the credit bureau. Although not confirmed by the credit bureaus, delinquent child support payments probably count against you the same as charge-offs. This is one negative on your credit report that also extracts a human emotion against you. Not paying child support really shows you as a "deadbeat" payee.

I had a client who had two child support claims against him. I really perceived him as a "deadbeat". However, upon questioning him, he was appalled that it showed up on his credit report. The problem was he had moved in and out of three states in a span of two years. The two previous states had made mistakes in transferring the money to the appropriate state. So in the eyes of two states he was a "deadbeat", even though he was paying each month as ordered. It was later cleared up and removed from his credit report. But anyone who reviewed his credit report and did not question him about it probably would have denied him credit.

Slow Pay on Accounts

Slow pays on an account also count against your credit score and how a lender evaluates your credit. If you are chronically late in paying your accounts what makes the lender think you will pay him on time? The lender may also feel that if you are already slow paying your bills, you don't need an additional loan. It might be the straw that will break the camel's back. The additional debt may take you from being a "slow pay" to a "don't pay".

The pattern of your slowness also plays a part in your credit score and how a lender evaluates your credit. If your credit report shows several late pays in a specific period of time a few years ago and none before or after, your credit score will not be seriously affected. Chances are there was a specific cause for the lateness. A lender will probably question you as to what was going on, and usually it will not hurt your chances of getting a loan and a good interest rate. Late pays within the year count against you more than late pays over a year ago.

The extent of your lateness is another big factor in determining your credit score and how the lender evaluates your credit. A few 30-day late pays on your credit does not affect your score too much. But, if you have been 60 days late or more on your accounts you will see a big drop in your score and also how the lender views your credit.

It would be to your advantage to contact your creditors as soon as you are disabled, lose your job, or for some other reason become unable to make your payments. Creditors are more understanding if they receive a call early that a payment cannot be made. Don't wait for the creditor to call you.

Time at Present Job
And
Time at Present Address

The time that you have spent at your present job and present home address shows your stability. Lenders like to see two plus years at both. The longer the better. If you hop from one job to another it usually means you have periods of time where your income could be zero. If you move around a lot and change home addresses frequently then the lender may not be able to locate you if you fail to pay on a loan.

Take two applicants, Jim and Fred. Both have credit reports that are identical, both applicants make the exact same pay on their jobs. The only difference is Jim has been at the same job for twenty years and owned his own house for fifteen years. Fred, on the other hand, has been on the job for one year and has lived at his current address for six months. Who gets the loan? Maybe both, depending on other factors, but if I had to choose between the two; I would give it to Jim. Without a doubt.

Ratio of Balances to Available Credit Lines

This refers to the amount of available credit you have left on revolving credit, such as credit cards or credit lines. It is calculated by dividing your total credit used by the total credit limits you have. For example, if your available credit is $10,000 and you have used $3,000, you would have used 30% of your available credit. The lower the percentage the better.

Number of Recent Inquiries

After you apply for a loan, the lender will usually pull a credit report. When he does this it is referred to as an inquiry. A few inquiries spread out over time will not harm your score and also will not effect a lenders decision on whether or not to grant you credit.

Inquiries become a problem when there are several on your credit report within a short amount of time. The lender then has to ask himself, "Why are there so many inquiries? Is this applicant shopping around that much in order to get the best rate? Or, do these other lenders know something I don't about the applicant's credit?" Too many recent inquiries will definitely throw up red flags to the lender. It also hurts your credit score because the computer model that calculates your score can't determine if you are shopping for a mortgage or automobile or if you are desperately trying to get a loan to keep from going into bankruptcy.

Number of Credit Lines

The number of credit lines you have open can affect your credit score. I don't feel that a lender who is evaluating your credit will put a lot of emphasis on the number of credit lines you have as much as the type of credit lines you have. Having a mortgage account on your credit is definitely a plus. Car loans are good also. What starts to count against you, both in score and in the evaluation by the lender, is having accounts with finance companies. In the eyes of the credit model and the lender, you should be borrowing from banks, not finance companies. They figure there must be a reason for you borrowing from a finance company.

Maybe your debt to income ratio will not allow you to borrow from a bank. Debt to income ratio or DTI is your debt divided by your income. For example, if you had $1,100 in debt and $2,500 in income, your DTI would be 44%. This level may prevent you from borrowing from a bank and may force you to borrow from a finance company. Finance companies typically have looser guidelines when it comes to credit and DTI. The trade-off is a higher interest rate.

My wife and I went shopping for a new kitchen table and entertainment center. The total price came to $1,500. The furniture store was offering one year, no interest if we opened up an account with them. I thought that was a great deal. As long as we could pay the $1,500 off within one year, the loan would be interest free. The furniture store had an agreement with Commercial Credit on all these types of purchases. Within a year, the loan was paid off in full, and we paid zero interest. But later, when I was applying for a loan from a bank, I was asked about that account. The bank wanted to know why I had a loan from a finance company. It was then that I found out how banks view finance companies. Even though I got a better deal going through a finance company, the bank felt I should have gone through them.

The credit model is designed to take points away from your score if you have accounts with finance companies. The reasoning from Fair Isaac is the same as banks. You should only borrow from banks, not finance companies.

If I had to do it all over again, I still would have gone the route of the finance company instead of a bank to finance that transaction. The cost to you may be a few points deducted from your credit score and an explanation to the lender. I would try to avoid having too many loans with finance companies if you can help it because you may find your credit score a lot lower than normal, and banks frowning at your credit.

Years You Have Had Credit in the Credit Bureau Database

The longer you have been in the credit bureau's database the better, as long as the accounts have been paid satisfactorily. Also, the longer you have had each account, the better, as long as they were paid on time. Suppose you had a Visa credit card for the last twelve years. This signals to a potential lender that you must have paid satisfactorily or the account would have been closed.

From a lender's viewpoint, the more years of credit on your credit report, the better he can get a feel for your pay history and your likelihood of repayment in the future.

From the credit-scoring model, the longer you are in the system and have accounts showing up, the better they can give a more accurate credit score on you. Which is the basic goal of Fair Isaac's credit scoring model, to accurately predict your likelihood of repayment on new loans.

Occupation, Homeowner, Age

Your occupation, being a homeowner, and your age are other factors that go into determining your credit score. However, this goes directly against the Equal Credit Opportunity Act (ECOA).

The ECOA clearly states that you cannot be discriminated against when applying for a loan. You should not be judged for credit on the basis of being a doctor or a janitor.

FICO reasons the better the profession the more likely the repayment of a loan. Also, a homeowner is more stable than a renter, and a retired person is more responsible than a twenty year old.

The Federal Trade Commission gave Fair Isaac permission to use these factors when determining credit scores. Is it right? I don't think so. Does the use of these factors present a clearer picture of the probability of repayment? As a representation on a whole, Yes.

Chapter Four

Reviewing Your Credit Report

We have discussed what factors make up your credit score and which items lenders pay close attention to and why. But what if your credit report is inaccurate? The *Federal Fair Credit Reporting Act* is your ally.

When you receive your credit report, you must sit down with a pencil and paper and review it (*do not write on your credit report*). You will be looking for any inaccurate items in your report.

Your credit report will list all creditors that have granted you credit or have placed judgements or liens against you, or placed you into collections, and any bankruptcies that you have filed. Each account will include the creditors name, your account number, credit limit, current balance, monthly payment, past pay history, current status of account, and date of last activity. You will also find all inquiries within the last two years.

Check everything about each account. Note any discrepancies, and check to see if an account is repeated elsewhere in your report. This can happen if an account has been transferred to another creditor.

Why do errors occur in your credit report? There are many reasons why. One could be that the creditor accidentally filed inaccurate information about your account to the credit bureau. You may have a common name that is easily confused. The reasons are endless.

Bankruptcy

If you have filed bankruptcy in the past, was the correct date listed as the filing date? Was it discharged or dismissed? What was the date of the discharge or dismissal? Was the bankruptcy discharge or dismissal over ten years ago? If so, it should not show up on your credit report.

If you never filed bankruptcy, you shouldn't have one listed.

Foreclosure

If you have, or had, a seriously delinquent mortgage you should have been notified if foreclosure proceedings had been filed against the property. If no notice is filed it should not be reported as a foreclosure on your credit report. I have not seen any mistakes on credit reports when it comes to foreclosures that shouldn't be listed. However, I am not saying it can't happen. I learned long ago, there is no telling what can show up on your credit report.

Judgements, Collections, Charge-Offs, Child Support, Slow Pay

Carefully review each account. Are judgements, collections, charge-offs, child support delinquencies, or slow pay on accounts accurate? If you have a judgement listed against you and you do not know whom it is for take a trip to the courthouse and research it. Usually, the person or company that filed judgement against you will be listed on your credit report.

Collections can be a little more difficult. If you had an account turned over to collections it may just state the collection company and the amount owed. It would be up to you to contact the collection company and find out what account was turned over to collections. There should only be one reference to each account being in collections on your credit report. Is the amount listed as being owed accurate? How old is the collection? Anything over seven years has to be removed.

Suppose you had an account with ABC Finance, and, due to lack of payment, it was turned over to a collection company. In your credit report you should only have one reference to that account being in collections. You should not have both ABC Finance and the collection company referring to the account as being in collections.

Charge-offs appear on your credit report as either I-9 or R-9. The "I" stands for "installment" and the "R" stands for "revolving". The "9" is the credit bureaus way of signifying charge-offs. A repossession would appear on your credit report as "I-8". The "8" is the credit bureaus way of signifying repossession.

Make sure the accounts charged-off are in fact yours. You may find an account charged-off or an automobile repossessed that you co-signed for. If this is the case you may be in for a surprise. **(See Co-signing for a Loan, page 37)**

The report may show an account charged-off or an automobile repossessed if you returned the item that secured the loan because it was a "lemon".

I had a client who, a couple of years prior, had purchased a car. After six months of constant problems with the car and the dealer refusing to fix it, the gentleman drove the car to the dealer, handed the dealer the keys, and told him exactly what he thought of the car and of him. My client told the dealer the car was a lemon and he wasn't going to make any more payments on a car that spent more time broken down than on the road.

Aside from the dealer possibly having his feelings hurt, he probably didn't care too much. You see, the bank had already paid the dealer. The bank doesn't care if the car doesn't run. All they care about is the fact they aren't getting a monthly payment anymore. When the car is sold at auction the money received will not be enough to pay off the outstanding loan against the car.

Anytime you have a defective product that you are making payments on, the best way to protect yourself is to continue to make your monthly payments while you dispute the product. This is not always the easiest way, especially if you have a "necessity" item such as a car with problems. But it is the only way to protect your credit. The exception to this is if you use a credit card to purchase an item that turns out to be defective.

If child support delinquencies show up on your report, make sure they are accurate. I have seen child support delinquencies later show up as judgements, which in fact had been paid out but never filed at the courthouse as being paid and satisfied.

Pay close attention to the pay history on each account. Especially, if an account shows you being late on payments. It is up to you to show proof you were not late for the months being specified on your report. Research your canceled checks or receipts for proof of payment. You do keep your canceled checks and paid receipts? Right?

Time at Present Job
Time at Present Address

If you are going to be in need of a loan in the near future, you may want to consider keeping your job and/or staying at the same address until after the loan is completed.

A few years ago, I received a promotion at my job. The promotion meant relocating to another state. Upon settling in I went to open a checking account with NationsBank. I applied for overdraft protection on the account. To my surprise I was denied. Not because of my credit score or information that was in my credit report but because I had been at my new location less than a week. I was finally granted the overdraft protection after I explained the reason for my move was a promotion with the same company. Their hesitation was based on the fact that I was new to the area and overdraft protection is basically an unsecured loan.

Ratio of Balances to Available Credit

The lower your balances are to your available credit the better. Do your balances match up to your records? I have seen in some cases where the current balance was reported incorrectly or the account hasn't been updated in several months. I have also seen on several occasions where an account was paid out but the balance at the time of being paid out is still showing. The creditor quit reporting to the bureau once the account was paid out. However, the creditor never notified the credit bureau that the account was paid out.

Number of Recent Inquiries

Review the list of recent inquiries. Inquiries can stay on your credit report for a maximum of two years. Do you have any inquiries older than two years? Who has inquired into your credit report? Did they have written authorization? That is an important question. If you do not remember giving written authorization make a note. Write down the address of the company inquiring. Your Experian report will list the addresses for each. Equifax and Trans Union do not report addresses.

Number of Credit Lines in Your Report

Review your credit report and make sure you can account for each credit line. Are any of the accounts reporting as open when in fact they are closed?

Number of Years You Have Credit in the Credit Bureau Database

This is something that can easily work to your advantage. Bad credit can only be reported to the credit bureaus for seven years, except for bankruptcy, which can report for ten years. If you have any delinquent accounts older than seven years make a note of them. If you have good credit accounts older than seven years leave them alone.

Viewing a Sample Credit Report

Let's review over the following credit report:

Please address all future correspondence to this address

EQUIFAX CREDIT INFORMATION SERVICES
P.O. BOX 740256
ATLANTA, GA 30374

(800) 303-6653

JOHN SMITH
111 NORTH MAIN STREET
ANYWHERE, USA 11111

DATE **12/5/99**
SOCIAL SECURITY NUMBER 111-11-1111
AGE 34

CREDIT HISTORY

Company Name	Account Number	Whose Acct.	Date Opened	Months Reviewed	Date of last Activity	High Credit	Terms	Items as of Date Reported			Date Reported
								Balance	Past Due	Status	
United Carolina Bank	564551	I	1/99	10	11/99	8658	179	7125		I-1	11/99
Sears	1564	J	6/94	65	10/99	4500		0		R-1	11/99
CBSG Finance	485618	I	2/99	9	4/99	1000	75	1100	525	I-5	11/99
	Charged Off Account										
First Bank	4324-4354	J	5/98	18	6/99	5400	254	4800		I-8	11/99
Auto	Involuntary Repossession										
Finance First	6797-986	J	4/98	23	11/99	2000	125	340	125	I-2	11/99
	***Prior Paying History	30(1)60(0)90(0)		11/99-I-2							
Peoples Bank	24332	J	2/99	9	11/99	1000	110	890	200	R-3	11/99
	***Prior Paying History	30(1)60(1)90(0)		10/99-I-2, 11/99-I-3							

*****PUBLIC RECORDS OR OTHER INFORMATION*****

BANKRUPTCY FILED CHP 7; CHATHAM COUNTY C; 2/93
DISCHARGED 5/93

Judgement Filed 11/97; CHATHAM COUNTY C; CASE OR OTHER ID NUMBER-97-CVM-353
DEFENDANT-SUBJ; AMOUNT $234; PLAINTIFF JANE DOE

*****ADDITIONAL INFORMATION*****

FORMER/OTHER ADDRESS BOX 402 PO, ANYWHERE, USA 11111

FORMER NAME JOHN C SMITH
JON SMITH

LAST REPORTED EMPL - DIRECTOR OF PURCHASING, HOUSE OF CHAMPIONS

FORMER EMPLOYMENT - UNKNOWN

***** COMPANIES THAT REQUESTED YOUR CREDIT HISTORY *****

12/5/99	EQUIFAX-DISCLOSURE	1/15/99	PRM ACE CREDIT CARDS
2/1/99	CBSG FINANCE	1/4/99	UNITED CAROLINA BANK
1/27/99	PEOPLES BANK	1/3/99	PRM SUPERIOR FINANCE

The upper half of the credit report is self-explanatory. It contains the name of the credit reporting agency and address, your name and address, the date, your social security number, and your age.

The important information about you is contained in the credit history section. You will notice many symbols used. The following are symbols used by Equifax:

Status	Timeliness of Payment
Type of Account	0= Approved not used; too new to rate
O= Open (entire balance due each month)	1= Paid as agreed
	2= 30+ days late
	3= 60+ days late
R= Revolving (payment amount variable)	4= 90+ days late
	5= pays or paid 120+ days past the due date; or collection account
I= Installment (fixed number of payments)	7= Making regular payments under wage earner plan or similar agreement
	8= Repossession
	9= Charged off to bad debt

Whose Account

J= Joint	M= Maker
I= Individual	C= Co-Maker/ Co-Signer
U= Undesignated	B= On behalf of another person
A= Authorized	S= Shared
T= Terminated	

Inquiries

PRM- This stands for a promotional inquiry. Your name and address were given to a potential lender so they could offer you an application for credit. A PRM inquiry stays on your credit file for six months. Your credit score is not affected by these inquiries.

AM or AR- These type of inquiries indicate a periodic review of your credit by one of your creditors. These inquiries stay on your credit file for six months.

EQUIFAX, ACIS, or UPDATE- These inquiries indicate Equifax's activity in response to your inquiry for a copy of your credit report or request for research.

The first account with United Carolina Bank shows the account number and that it is an individual account. It was first opened in January of 1999. The activity on the account has been reviewed for ten months, with the last date of activity being November 1999. The high credit on the account is $8,658. The payment due each month is $179. The current balance is $7,125. The account has been paid on time and reflects an I-1 status, with the last date reported on this account being November 1999.

The Sears account is a little different in that it shows it being a joint account. There are at least two people responsible for payment on this account, usually a spouse. The status reflects a R-1. Meaning it is a revolving account with payments in good standing at the present time.

The CBSG Finance account reflects a past due amount of $525 and a status of I-5. Below the account number you will see "Charged Off Account". This reflects that payment is severely delinquent and the lender has written the account off as a loss. The status of I-5 shows an installment account past due at least 120 days.

First Bank shows a joint account for a car loan that has been repossessed. The status shows an I-8.

Finance First shows a joint account that is $125 past due. The status is I-2, meaning 30 days past due. Below the account you will see the pay history. There has been only one time the account was past due. That was November 1999.

Peoples Bank shows an account $200 past due and a R-3 rating.

Below the account you will see the pay history. You will note in October 1999 the account was 30 days past due and in November 1999 the account went 60 days past due. Thus, the R-3 rating.

In the public record section, you will see a chapter 7 bankruptcy filed in February of 1993. It was discharged in May of 1993. You also see the county in which the bankruptcy was filed.

A judgment was also filed in November 1997, at the Chatham County courthouse. It shows the case docket number as well as the person filing the judgment and the judgment amount.

Under "additional information" you will see former addresses and former names. You may have different variations of your name in this section as you see for John Smith. Also reported is current and former employment.

The inquiry section shows everyone who has inquired about John Smith's credit. You will see one inquiry from Equifax in response to John Smith's inquiry for a copy of his credit report. There were also inquiries from companies John applied to. As evidenced by the accounts showing up in the credit history section. Also, PRM inquiries from Ace Credit Cards and Superior Finance report as a result of promotional purposes.

Chapter Five

Starting the Cleanup Process

Now that you have reviewed your credit report and made notes of all errors, it is time to get down to business. One important fact to keep in mind: You cannot change your FICO score, you can only change the information used in determining your FICO score.

There are several rules to go by when disputing your credit report to either the credit bureaus or creditors.

1. Always tell the truth when disputing your credit report. As long as you believe your credit report contains errors, you are free to dispute any item. In some states it may be against the law to lie when disputing your credit report.
2. The credit bureau or creditor needs to know exactly what you are disputing. You either challenge a listing as "not mine" or "not late". If you are not clear about what you are contesting, the credit bureau or creditor will return your letter.
3. In your letter to the credit bureau and/or creditors, explain the desired outcome of their investigation.
4. What are your reasons for the dispute?
5. What is your evidence for the dispute?
6. Do not flood the credit bureau or creditors with disputes. Some credit repair companies advise sending several letters disputing the same item

with hopes one of the letters will not get a response. New laws have been passed discouraging multiple mailings of the same dispute in a short period of time.

7. Your disputes should be typed not handwritten.

When disputing information contained in your credit report to credit bureaus you should include:

Full name
Birth date
Social Security number
Current address
Former addresses for the last five years
Photocopy of drivers license, showing current address
Photocopy of Social Security card

When disputing items to creditors be careful whom you give your address to. You do not want to give out certain information if you will be trying to negotiate a settlement on a collection or charge-off. More on that later.

Inquiries

Remember, I said all inquiries must have your written authorization. I'm not saying that it is against the law to pull credit without a written authorization. But it will work to your advantage if they do not have your written authorization on file. Prepare a letter to each creditor who had inquired into your credit asking them to remove their inquiry. What you are doing is challenging the creditor as to whether they had proper authorization to pull your credit.

Make sure you send your letter *Certified Mail Return Receipt Requested* and keep track of when you mailed the letter. The creditor has approximately thirty days to respond to your letter. Some creditors may remove the inquiry out of courtesy; some may remove it because they don't feel like going into their files to see if they actually had proper authorization to pull your credit. There may also be some creditors who will ignore you altogether. After a reasonable amount of time with no response from the inquiring creditors, you win. Regardless of the fact that they may have proper authorization on file from you, they are bound by the Fair Credit Reporting Act to remove your inquiry. At this point you should call the creditor and demand they remove your inquiry.

State you do not remember giving written authorization for the inquiry. You wrote a letter to the company over thirty days ago. You have proof they received the letter over thirty days ago. They did not respond to the letter. They are bound by the Fair Credit Reporting Act. If they don't remove the inquiry immediately you will complain to the State Banking Commission (if they are regulated by the Banking Commission. Find out who they are regulated by first, before you call).

You should be able to remove some of your inquiries by using this tactic and add a few points back to your credit score. **(See page 60 for sample letter)**

Slow Pays

The easiest way to resolve disputed late pays is to research your records and find either a canceled check or a receipt showing proof of payment. Make a copy of the evidence and, along with a letter, send the evidence *Certified Mail Return Receipt Requested.* You can also ask the company to mail you a printout of your pay history. Again, the company has thirty days to respond to your request. The company may send back a printed pay history showing you as being late. At this point you can send a letter to the credit bureau stating you are disputing the creditor's claim of being late and send a copy of the original letter you sent to the creditor, the printed pay history from the company, and your proof of payment. The credit bureau will now attempt to verify the claim. If the credit bureau can verify that you were indeed correct, they will remove the negative entry. (see chapter 11 for samples)

Bankruptcy

If you noted discrepancies in your credit report concerning your bankruptcy; contact your trustee. You and your trustee should have copies of everything concerning your bankruptcy. You can mail a letter to the trustee, *Certified Mail Return Receipt Requested*, requesting the trustee update the status of your bankruptcy, or report it has been discharged or dismissed.

Foreclosure

If your credit report shows an inaccurate foreclosure against you, contact the lender. Request a pay history on your account and any information they have showing evidence of foreclosure proceedings against you. While waiting for their response gather your evidence showing you were never in foreclosure. Review the documentation you receive. Submit a letter, *Certified Mail Return Receipt Requested,* and proof you were never in foreclosure. The company has approximately thirty days, upon receipt of your letter, to respond to your demand to have the foreclosure listing removed from your credit report.

Collections

A duplicate reference to an account in collections can easily result in the removal of one of the referring accounts. As mentioned before, if XYZ Finance company has placed you into collections with ABC Collection Company, then there can only be one reference to the account being in collections. It has to be either with XYZ or ABC. Simply send a letter, *Certified Mail Return Receipt Requested,* to XYZ Finance and demand they remove their reference to the account being in collections on the credit bureau since they have now assigned the account to a collection company. If they do not respond, send a letter to the credit bureau stating your claim.

You may have collections that are accurate. If so, there is still a way to improve your situation. You can negotiate a settlement on the account in exchange for a removal of listing on your credit report. Your chance of success for a full removal of the listing is 50/50.

Here are a few tips for negotiating a settlement on any collections or charge-offs:

1. Creditors make their money from collecting money from customers, not from reporting negative information about the customer.
2. Collection agencies are usually more agreeable to remove any negative information about you than banks and credit card companies.
3. You need the collection company to remove their listing entirely upon receipt of the settlement and also have the original creditor either remove their listing entirely or change the listing to paid as agreed. Some companies may tell you they have no power in having the original creditor

change their listing. This may be true. However, both the collection agency and the original creditor want their money. If the wording of your listing or the removal of your listing stands in the way of receiving money, they may be willing to see it your way.

4. A collection company may tell you they have an agreement with the credit bureau that they will not, in exchange for a settlement, remove a collection listing. You can remind the collection company you know they can contact the credit bureau and tell them the collection listing was done in error and not as a result of a settlement.

5. Never tell a collection company your phone number, where you work, bank or, if you have moved, your new home address. If the settlement negotiating falls through the collection company may seek a garnishment against you. Knowing you are employed and have a bank account may give them incentive not to negotiate and instead seek garnishment of wages against you. If you own a house, they may decide they would rather just have a lien against you.

6. Never pay a settlement with a personal check. Your personal check will have your account number on it. Pay with a money order or cashier's check from a different place than your bank.

7. Keep your copy of the money order or cashier's check in a safe spot. This is your proof you actually paid.

8. Anything less than "paid as agreed" doesn't help your cause any. If the collection listing later states "settlement on account", you will not have improved your credit score.

9. No matter how much money you have, you will still portray yourself to the collection company as the poorest person on earth who just happened to come into a couple of bucks. If the collection company thinks you have money they will not be so quick to settle. However, if they believe this is their one chance to get some money they usually will be quick to start negotiating.

Contact the collection company and explain you have some problems with your credit and you want to take care of them. But, you have limited money to accomplish this. Tell the company you can send in a settlement for half of the amount due. In exchange, you want a full removal from your credit report of any reference of a collection. But, you will not mention the full removal until you get a little bit into the negotiating.

This technique works the same with charge-offs. Simply negotiate a settlement. One thing to keep in mind is collections and charge-offs represent lost revenue for the creditor. You are offering to make restitution for this lost money. Another thing to keep in mind is that time is on your side. The more time that has passed the more likely an agent is to work with you. Don't expect an agent to be willing to work with you if your account recently went into collections or was charged-off. If, however, your account has been in collections or charged-off for a few years, the agent may be very willing to settle with you.

Negotiating is an art. The more practice you have the better you become. But for the novice, knowing the rules before you begin can be a big help.

A few rules:

Is the debt secured or unsecured?

If the debt is secured by something (auto, TV, Stereo, Etc.) the creditor has more leverage than you. The creditor could seize the property and sell in order to collect on the debt.

If the debt is unsecured you have more leverage. The creditor has nothing to secure his claim with. Thus, you have more bargaining power.

What is the size of the debt?

The smaller the size of the debt, the greater your odds of getting it reduced and settled. A creditor will not devote a lot of time and effort trying to collect on a couple of hundred dollars.

One drawback to a small balance trying to be negotiated is there also isn't a whole lot of incentive for the collector to devote much time trying to negotiate a small debt.

What is the age of the debt and history of repayment?

The older the debt, the better your chances at getting a reduced settlement. If you have not made any payments on the account in a while then the collector isn't anticipating any more payments and has already written the debt off as a loss.

If you first offer a settlement of 50%, the collection agent may counter that he can only accept 90% of the balance as a settlement. He may be limited in how much of the debt he can write off or he may think you can offer a little more. In the first round of negotiating he is willing to wait a little bit. Turn the tables around to his side. He has a person calling in concerned about his/her credit and wants to make amends. He knows he can go down more on the settlement offer but he doesn't want to leave any money on the table. The more he collects the more he earns in commission.

At this point you may ask to speak to his supervisor. Be polite. Nobody likes dealing with someone being rude. Remember, you get more flies with honey than with vinegar. Explain your situation again. You made mistakes in the past and now you want to correct them. You have several collections with different collection agencies that you are trying to settle. What is the lowest they can settle this account for?

The supervisor may then counter with 75% settlement on the account. At this point you may decide that is as far as they will go down on the settlement offer. This is when you make your concession. You tell the supervisor you want to settle at 50% but you will settle at 75% on one condition. That condition is, you want a letter from the collection company and the original creditor, stating that upon receipt of the 75% (or whatever percentage is agreed upon), the collection listing will be removed. And the original creditor will state your account "paid as agreed" and remove any late pay statements.

This is usually when the collection company will start balking. "Oh, we can't do that!!!" or "The original creditor will not allow us to do that." Or "Absolutely Not!!!"

At this point you calmly explain that while you want to clear up your credit there is no incentive for you to settle on this account if you can't come to an agreement on full removal of the negative listing. You have no job, no assets and you know the negative listing will come off after seven years unless they refile the claim. But, they will be wasting their time refiling because if you haven't paid after seven years what makes them think you will repay in another seven years. Again, do not come across as defensive, arrogant, or rude. Rather, you have some money you can send to them but you have to have full removal of the collection listing. **(See page 64 for a sample letter)**

They may still refuse your request. Tell them you appreciate their time and you are sorry a settlement couldn't be reached. Call them back about a week later and ask if they would reconsider. Business may be slow at the collection company and they may now be willing to settle for your original demands. If not, call back a month later, and try again. There may be a new supervisor on duty who is eager to deal. Remember, time is on your side.

If the collection was a result of a bad debt to a local doctor or some other small or local business you may find you can be successful in approaching the original creditor about having the collection listing removed. A collection company deals with all kinds of customers and hears all the sob stories when trying to collect on a debt. However, when you approach the local doctor, explain your situation and that you are trying to right yourself, your credit; and you have money you want to give to him. You might extract that compassionate side out of the doctor and he will call the collection company and instruct them that the listing was an error and should be removed.

If a settlement can be reached will the collection agent put the agreement in writing? They may promise they will remove the negative listing but not offer anything in writing or say they cannot put that offer in writing. Do not take a promise on this one. Why? Who is to say the collection agent that you have been dealing with will be there after you have sent in your money? What if he quits, gets fired or suddenly comes down with amnesia? If you don't have an agreement in writing, you don't have anything.

If you want to pay off the collection account but the collection company will not agree to remove the listing you have a couple other options. Not that they really help your score but a prospective lender may look a little more favorably at your credit when deciding whether or not to grant you credit based on your credit itself and not your credit score.

The collection company may only agree to list your account as "settled". This will still be a negative to your credit report but it may show to a prospective lender you were concerned about your credit to a degree to pay off the debt. This should be a last resort because this listing really is of no benefit to you.

Another drawback to this type of listing is it starts the seven-year listing all over again on your credit report. Negative information can only be listed on your credit report for seven years (bankruptcy is ten years) from the date of last activity. If you have an account that has been in collections for five years already, you will have two years remaining before it drops off your credit report. If you pay off the account and the creditor will only list is as "settled" then for the next seven years you will have that collection account on your credit report and the next to it will be "settled". Where is the incentive for you to pay out the collection? There is none. This is what you want to explain to the collection agent.

Ratio of Balances to Available Credit Lines

Your credit score is improved when you have a large difference between what you owe on your credit lines and the amount of your credit lines. If you are applying for a new credit card and the creditor sees you are just about maxed out on all your other credit cards; he is going to feel you are likely to become a bankruptcy candidate. He will feel you are asking for a credit card or a loan because you have used up your existing credit lines and need more. This may or may not be the case.

A lender feels warm and fuzzy when he sees an applicant who owes less than half of the credit line granted on the credit report (to get more points towards your credit score keep a ratio of less than 25% owing versus credit available). He gets the sense the applicant has a grasp on his/her finances and isn't dependent on credit cards.

If you are maxed out on your credit lines or owe more than 25% on your credit lines, there is a simple solution. Providing you have paid as agreed the creditor may be willing to grant you additional credit. It can be as simple as a phone call. Of course, this advice isn't given with the intent for you to go and borrow more against your credit cards. Doesn't it look better on your credit report for you to owe $2,000 when the credit line is $5,000 rather than a week ago when you owed $2,000 and the credit line was for $2,500. Nothing in your personal financial life has changed but your financial profile on your credit report has improved.

Number of Credit Lines on your Report

Your credit score and how a lender evaluates your credit is effected by the number of credit lines reporting to the credit bureaus. I was once turned down for credit because I had too many open accounts on my credit. It did not matter the date of last activity was a few years ago and the balance was zero. The lender viewed it as I could go and borrow at any time, thus possibly putting repayment of his loan in jeopardy. His suggestion was I close some of the accounts.

If you have credit lines open that you have not used in a while and have no intention of using then it may be wise to close those accounts. My wife and I had a furniture store credit card that we opened when we first got married. It was a small chain store that reported to the credit bureaus. A few years later we moved out of state to an area where this chain does not operate. If there isn't a store where we are located then why have the account open? The only thing it does for us is increase the chance that someone may steal our credit card and go to that store and fraudulently buy merchandise with our credit card.

Your 100-Word statement

Federal law allows you to make a statement concerning your credit history or an account up to 100 words on your credit report. The reason for this is anyone checking into your credit can get a brief look at your side of the story. Maybe you were sick or laid off work a couple of years ago and a few accounts became delinquent. Maybe there was an account delinquent because you disputed the validity of the merchandise securing the account.

This comes from personal experience of viewing credit reports. I have never read a statement that resulted in changing my original opinion of the credit report. What a statement does do to your credit report is eliminate the credit score. I don't know why but it does. The disadvantage to including a statement about your credit is if a creditor relies heavily on your credit score whether to grant you a loan or not you will most likely be denied the loan.

What the creditor or credit bureau does in response to your claim

A creditor or credit bureau must respond to your claim within a reasonable amount of time, usually thirty days. Here are a few things a creditor or credit bureau can do in response to your claim.

No response at all.
A letter asking for more information.
A rejection letter based on the timing of your dispute. (They may have just received a letter from you disputing the same item)
A rejection letter on the grounds that the dispute is "frivolous or irrelevant".
A rejection based on the grounds that the credit bureau believes you are manipulating the system. (They may feel that you are attempting unethical credit repair by bombarding them with dispute letters or that you won't dispute this type of rejection)

A letter announcing that your investigation has begun.
A letter announcing that your dispute has been forwarded to the appropriate credit bureau.
A new credit report showing the results of an investigation.

If you are not getting the desired results for your efforts, you may want to send another letter with one of the following phrases or use a sample found on page 62:

"I've contacted a lawyer and am considering legal action."
"I will be filing a complaint with the Federal Trade Commission."
"I am preparing letters to my state senators and representatives."

By including one of these phrases you show the creditor/credit bureau that you are not going away and that you are aware of your rights.

If you do want to register a complaint with the FTC, you may write:

Federal Trade Commission
Pennsylvania Ave. and Sixth St., N.W.
Washington, D.C. 20580

Chapter Six

Co-Signing a Loan

It is difficult to say no when asked to co-sign on a loan for a child, close relative, or friend. After all, this is how you probably started establishing your own credit. There is nothing wrong with co-signing but make sure you are aware of the consequences that are associated with it.

According to the Federal Trade Commission, creditors are required to give you notice that explains your obligations.

The co-signers notice states:

You are being asked to guarantee this debt. Think carefully before you do. If the borrower does not pay the debt, you will have to. Be sure you can afford to pay if you have to, and that you want to accept this responsibility.

You may have to pay up to the full amount of the debt if the borrower does not pay. You may also have to pay late fees or collection costs, which increase this amount.

The creditor can collect this debt from you without first trying to collect from the borrower. The creditor can use the same collection methods against you that can be used against the borrower, such as suing you, garnishing your wages, etc. If this debt is ever in default, that fact may become a part of your credit record.*

This notice is not the contract that makes you liable for the debt.

**Depending on your state, this may not apply. If state law forbids a creditor from collecting from a cosigner without first trying to collect from the primary debtor, this sentence may be crossed out or omitted altogether.*

Before you cosign for a loan, consider the following:

1) Can you afford to pay the loan if you're asked or forced to pay.
2) Understand that if you collateralize any of your own property for a loan you may lose it if the loan defaults.
3) Will the lender contact you if the borrower misses a payment? Will the lender be willing to put that agreement in writing?
4) Get copies of all the important papers, especially the loan contract.
5) Know your cosigner rights- these vary from state to state.
6) Understand that if there are delinquent payments your credit profile could be adversely affected.
7) You may also be held responsible for late fees, and attorney fees.

Repossession

You found the car you like. You finance $8000 for five years at a payment of $180 per month. You make the payments like clockwork for the first three years but then you are laid off from work. Next thing you know, you are four months past due on your car payment. You've been getting notices and phone calls concerning your delinquency. One day you go to check the mail and notice your car is gone. The "repo" man has been to your house. The bank has repossessed your car.

The bank has taken your car and sold it at auction for $2000. You get a notice in the mail a couple of weeks later that you still have an outstanding bill of $2300. If you owed $4000 on the car before the repossession and the bank only received $2000 at the auction for the car; that would leave $2000 for the balance remaining and $300 for attorney fees. The end result is you have no car and still owe money on the car. Not only that, but your credit report will now have an I-8 (repossession) for the status of your car loan.

Repossession of automobiles, as well as other personal items, is a legal practice used against delinquent borrowers. Repossession is a bank's last defense against delinquent borrowers. Believe it or not, a bank is not in the business of owning cars. They would rather lend the money.

There are other items that can be repossessed as well. Furniture, boats, TVs, and stereos are other items that if not paid satisfactorily can be repossessed.

Chapter Seven

Effects of Divorce

Divorce can have a devastating effect on one's credit. Even if the divorce is an amicable one. Whenever any of the emotions of divorce get involved, the effect on credit and finances can be grueling. Before the divorce, you usually have two incomes supporting the household. After a divorce, the incomes are supporting two households (2 house payments, 2 phone bills, 2 electricity bills, etc.).

The biggest cause of delinquent credit after a divorce is from misinformation in the divorce papers. The divorce papers may spell out who is responsible for which jointly held accounts. However, the creditor doesn't care who is responsible now in the eyes of the divorce court. When an account is signed jointly, both signers are equally responsible for repayment of the loan until the account is satisfied in full. If one spouse is elected to pay an account and doesn't, then the other spouse is held equally liable. Divorce changes nothing.

You may take legal action against your ex-spouse for not following the divorce decree. By then, the damage is done by to your credit.

If you are worried that your ex-spouse may not pay his/her portion on a jointly held account, then you may want to take steps to ensure that there aren't any late pays to the account. If it is a jointly held credit card, you should close the account. This will keep your ex-spouse from running up any charges on the card. If you want to keep the card you may ask to open an individual account instead.

On joint installment loans, you may want to call the company and explain that you are getting divorced and that your spouse is responsible for the account via divorce decree. However, you understand that you are equally responsible for the account in the creditors eyes, and that you would like to be notified if the account approaches delinquency. Most creditors would be more than happy to notify you if the account approaches delinquency stage. It may not help your situation if you don't have the money to make the payment or if your ex-spouse still refuses to pay, but at least you won't have any surprises.

Be careful on any accounts to which your ex-spouse is an authorized user. You and only you are responsible for the account; however, your ex-spouse can still use the account. A spiteful spouse may run up an account and you would be in for a surprise when the bill comes. Contact the creditor and request that the account be switched to a "single user".

If you have already been a victim of your ex-spouse ruining your credit you should contact the creditors and explain your circumstances. Creditors may be willing to work with you. You may be able to renegotiate the loans into an affordable payment for you. Remember, the creditor wants to get paid. If they have a customer who is that concerned about their credit then they will be more than willing to work with you.

Chapter Eight

An Alternative to Consumer Credit Counseling

The first thing you should do before you fall behind on your bills is contact your creditors. Explain your situation (you were just laid-off, disabled, spouse ill or died, etc.). Any creditor appreciates being called before delinquency occurs. If you think your situation will only be temporary, tell your creditor that. Ask to have your debt restructured. Maybe the lender will change the due date from the first of the month to the fifteenth. But, very important, explain to the creditor you don't want your credit rating affected. Will the creditor post the account as "payment deferred" or some other type of negative rating? Negotiate and get it in writing.

If you anticipate your situation being more long-term, tell the creditor that. You may want to tell the creditor you are considering bankruptcy. Creditors hate that word. Why? The creditor might not get any money if you file bankruptcy. Start negotiating. Will the creditor stop interest from accruing and set up a payment arrangement for you? Their proposal might be higher than what you can afford. Especially, if you have other creditors you need to talk to also. Evaluate all proposals before you commit. If the proposals are still too high for you, start contacting your creditors and see who can lower their payment plan.

You can negotiate how an account will be listed on your credit report. What is your negotiating tool? If the creditor says they can only list the account with the credit bureaus as the account being in some type of plan or payment deferred, does it help you? No. It will show up as a negative whether it is listed as "in payment plan" or "bankruptcy". You want to negotiate the account being listed as "paid as agreed" and a new loan set up with the terms you just agreed upon.

What have you done here? You have accomplished the same thing Consumer Credit Counseling Services (CCCS) can do for you only better. If you enter into a plan with CCCS, your accounts will be listed as "in consumer credit counseling". Which to some lenders is just as bad as bankruptcy.

Who is CCCS? They are a nationwide association helping financially troubled consumers repay their existing bills through a debt repayment plan. They advertise themselves as a non-profit organization. Are they truly non-profit? It depends on who you ask. CCCS is backed in part by the creditors themselves. In essence the creditors have their own bill collector. Creditors also give back a portion of the money you pay in CCCS's repayment plan back to CCCS.

Chapter Nine

Fair Debt Collection

If you use credit cards, owe money on a personal loan, or are paying on a home mortgage, you are a "debtor". If you fall behind in repaying your creditors, or an error is made on your accounts, you may be contacted by a "debt collector".

You should know that in either situation the Fair Debt Collection Practice Act requires that debt collectors treat you fairly by prohibiting certain methods of debt collection. Of course, the law does not forgive any legitimate debt you owe.

The following provides answers to commonly asked questions to help you understand your rights under the Fair Debt Collection Practices Act.

What debts are covered?

Personal, family, and household debts are covered under the Act. This includes money owed for the purchase of an automobile, for medical care, or for charge accounts.

Who is a debt collector?

A debt collector is any person, other than the creditor, who regularly collects debts owed to others. Under a 1986 amendment to the Fair Debt

Collection Practices Act, this includes attorneys who collect debts on a regular basis.

How may a debt collector contact you?

A collector may contact you in person, by mail, telephone, telegram, or FAX. However, a debt collector may not contact you at unreasonable times or places, such as before 8 a.m. or after 9 p.m., unless you agree. A debt collector also may not contact you at work if the collector knows that your employer disapproves.

Can you stop a debt collector from contacting you?

You may stop a collector from contacting you by writing a letter to the collection agency telling them to stop. Once the agency receives your letter, they may not contact you again except to say there will be no further contact. Another exception is that the agency may notify you if the debt collector or the creditor intends to take some specific action.

May a debt collector contact any person other than you concerning your debt?

If you have an attorney, the debt collector may not contact anyone other than your attorney. If you do not have an attorney, a collector may contact other people, but only to find out where you live and work. Collectors usually are prohibited from contacting such permissible third parties more than once. In most cases, the collector is not permitted to tell anyone other than you and your attorney that you owe money.

What is the debt collector required to tell you about the debt?

Within five days after you are first contacted, the collector must send you a written notice telling you the amount of money you owe; the name of the creditor to whom you owe the money; and what action to take if you believe you do not owe the money.

May a debt collector continue to contact you if you believe you do not owe money?

A collector may not contact you if, within 30 days after you are first contacted, you send the collection agency a letter stating you do not owe money. However, a collector can renew collection activities if you are sent proof of the debt, such as a copy of a bill for the amount owed.

What types of debt collection practices are prohibited?

Harassment. Debt collectors may not harass, oppress, or abuse any person. For example, debt collectors may not:

Use threats of violence or harm against the person, property, or reputation;

Publish a list of consumers who refuse to pay their debts (except to a credit bureau);

Use obscene or profane language;

Repeatedly use the telephone to annoy someone;

Telephone people without identifying themselves;

Advertise your debt.

False statements. Debt collectors may not use any false statements when collecting a debt. For example, debt collectors may not:

Falsely imply that they are attorneys or government representatives;

Falsely imply that you have committed a crime;

Falsely represent that they operate or work for a credit bureau;

Misrepresent the amount of your debt;

Misrepresent the involvement of an attorney in collecting a debt;

Indicate that papers being sent to you are legal forms when they are not; Indicate that papers being sent to you are not legal forms when they are.

Debt collectors also may not state that:

You will be arrested if you do not pay your debt;

They will seize, garnish, attach, or sell your property or wages, unless the collection agency or creditor intends to do so, and it is legal to do so;

Actions, such as a lawsuit, will be taken against you, which legally may not be taken, or which they do not intend to take.

Debt collectors may not:

Give false credit information about you to anyone;

Send you anything that looks like an official document from a court or government agency when it is not;

Use a false name.

Unfair practices. Debt collectors may not engage in unfair practices in attempting to collect a debt. For example, collectors may not:

Collect any amount greater than your debt, unless allowed by law;

Deposit a post-dated check prematurely;

Make you accept collect calls or pay for telegrams;

Take or threaten to take your property unless this can be done legally;
Contact you by postcard.

What control do you have over payment of debts?

If you owe more than one debt, any payment you make must be applied to the debt you indicate. A debt collector may not apply a payment to any debt you believe you do not owe.

What can you do if you believe a debt collector violated the law?

You have the right to sue a collector in a state or federal court within one year from the date you believe the law was violated. If you win, you may recover money for the damages you suffered. Court costs and attorney's fees also can be recovered. A group of people also may sue a debt collector and recover money for damages up to $500,000, or one percent of the collector's net worth, whichever is less.

Where can you report a debt collector for an alleged violation of the law?

Report any problems you have with a debt collector to your state Attorney General's office and the Federal Trade Commission. Many states also have their own debt collection laws and your Attorney General's office can help you determine your rights.

If you have questions about the *Fair Debt Collection Practices Act*, or your rights under the Act, write: *Correspondence Branch, Federal Trade Commission, Washington, D.C. 20580.* Although the FTC generally cannot intervene in individual disputes, the information you provide may indicate a pattern of possible law violations requiring action by the Commission.

How to handle a debt collector

1. Don't say anything!!!
2. Do not give out any information!!! The more information the debt collector has about you the more ammunition he has. The only thing you should ask for is their company name, the collector's name, and their business address.
3. Never admit to owing the debt. Whether you owe it or not is not relevant yet. I am not advocating not paying your bills. However, it is up

to the debt collector to prove that you owe it. Let them earn their money.
4. Do not confirm your job status. Especially if you have changed jobs. If they know where you work then they can call you there. They will try trick questions to make you stumble into giving them the information that they are after. Remember, they are professionals.
5. Do not pay any money by check. Pay by cash or money order only. If you pay by check then they have all the bank information they need (i.e. your account number).
6. Do not send a postdated check. This gives them your bank information.
7. Tell them you don't want to be contacted again with the exception of written proof that you owe the debt.
8. Send the letter on page 51. Keep a copy for your records.

What a debt collector can do.

1. A debt collector can contact you (via mail, phone, or message) up to three times per week unless you send a letter with return receipt (this proves the collection company received your letter).
2. A debt collector can call your relatives or neighbors to have them give you a message unless you send a letter with return receipt.
3. They must send you proof upon written request. Which you will have done by sending a letter with return receipt.
4. They can sue you. But the likelihood of this happening diminishes the less they know about you (job status, whether you have the ability to repay or not).

A debt collector may try different approaches. Some may seem as if they are your ally. Hoping that you will open up to them and share needed information. This is their job. Their job is to get you to pay back a debt.

Again, I am not saying that it is okay not to pay your bills. I just want you to know your rights if you are ever in this situation.

The following letter is an example of a letter that you can send to a debt collector. You do not want your signature anywhere on it because it may be too easy to copy, print your name instead.

Date:

From (your name and address):

To (debt company and collector):

Re (the account number of the debts):

Dear (name of collection company):

This letter serves as notice that under the Fair Debt Collection Practices Act I demand that you no longer contact me in any way from the date you receive this letter. Any contact will constitute a damage of $1,000 per incident. Additionally, I dispute the debt entirely. This letter also serves as notice of an official request of proof that I owe this debt as defined in the Fair Debt Collection Practices Act. I am requesting a copy of a document bearing my signature obligating myself to this alleged debt.

Sincerely,

____
(Print your name, do not sign it)

Sample letter against harassment from debt collectors

Date __________

Your Name
Address
City, State, Zip
Account
Account#

To: Customer Relations
Name of Business
Address
City, State, Zip

Subject: Complaint of Harassment
I am currently unable to pay my obligation in full because ________________________. However, under the protection of the Fair Debt Collection Practices Act, I am entitled to certain rights. Your collection company is in violation of the law by their actions stated as follows____. I will forgo legal action in small claims court for punitive damages. In return, I expect your written assurance that you and your agency will permanently cease all efforts to collect this obligation as well as remove all negative information regarding this account in my credit file. I appreciate your prompt reply.

Your Name
Signature

Spouse's Name (if joint account)
Signature (if joint account)

CC: Federal Trade Commission
State Collection Agency Licensing Board
Collection Agency (Name)
***Note**: If the account is a joint account, make sure to include your spouse. If not it is possible the collection company may still try to collect from your spouse.*

Chapter Ten

File Segregation and Rebuilding Your Credit

File Segregation

Have you seen these headlines?

> "Credit problems? No problem!"
> "Create a new credit identity-legally."
> "We can erase your bad credit-100% guaranteed"
> "We can remove bankruptcies, judgements, liens, and bad debt from your credit report permanently"

Sounds very tempting especially if you have bad credit and keep getting turned down every time you apply for a loan.

There are many companies across the country that are advertising these claims. What they are proposing is called File Segregation.

"File Segregation" is illegal. What these companies have you do is apply for an Employer Identification Number EIN) for the Internal Revenue Service. An EIN is used by businesses to report financial information to the IRS or Social Security Administration. EINs resemble social security numbers, so a creditor wouldn't know if it is a social security number or not. After receiving an EIN, customers are told to apply for new credit using the EIN instead of their own social security number.

The reason that it is illegal is that it is a crime for any consumer to misrepresent his or her social security number and it is also a crime to obtain an EIN from the IRS under false pretenses. Consumers may find themselves charged with mail or wire fraud if they use the mail or telephone to apply for credit and provide false information. Consumers may also be sued for civil fraud under many state laws.

There are no quick fixes here to repair your credit if the information contained on your credit report is accurate. Only time can repair it. Here are a few tips to keep in mind if you are approached about or considering "credit repair":

* File segregation is illegal.
* Be wary of companies that offer an immediate solution to your credit problems.
* Never do business with any credit service organization without first Checking with your State Attorney General office or the Better Business Bureau.
* Credit repair companies can't legally do anything that you can't do yourself.
* If you feel you have been a victim of a credit repair scam, contact your Attorney General.

Rebuilding Your Credit

You should now have an understanding of your credit report, how to correct errors contained in your report, and the importance of good credit. It's now time to start the rebuilding process of your credit. This is not something that can be improved overnight but there are a few things that you can do to set it on the right track.

One of the easiest methods is to apply for a secured credit card through a reputable issuing bank. A deposit made by you into their bank secures a secured credit card. The bank will grant you a credit limit based on the amount of your deposit. The bank will report this account to the credit bureau just as any other account (ask the bank if they report to the credit bureaus first). Over time as you repay on time they may, and usually do, increase your credit limit without you having to deposit additional money into the bank. Insist that the bank give you the option of switching to a regular credit card later if all monthly payments have been made on time when you first apply. Also, find a bank that doesn't charge a fee when first opening a secured credit card account. Try to keep your balances as low as possible and make sure you pay on time. Do not max out the card because that will lower your credit score.

Another method is to round up as much cash as you can (at least a thousand dollars), even if you have to save it up for a few months. Open a savings account and deposit the money at a local bank or credit union. After a week make an appointment to see the branch manager. You don't want to see a loan officer for this. Loan officers come and go. Branch managers tend to stay and you may need him/her to remember you later.

Explain that you are trying to rebuild your credit and would like to borrow against money you already have with the bank (the money you used to open the savings account a week ago). The bank will love this idea because they cannot lose. They have your money on deposit that they can use as collateral in case you don't pay the loan. You want the term of the loan to be for at least one year.

The next step is to take that money that you receive as part of the loan and go repeat this method at another bank. Do this a total of three times. Take the proceeds that you receive from the last loan and put that into a separate checking account. Keep this separate from your regular checking account. You can use this money to help pay the monthly payments on the three loans you have taken out. Do not become delinquent on any of these loans. If you do you will defeat the whole purpose of trying to rebuild your credit.

The longer you keep these accounts open the more it improves your score. At the end of the year you would have three paid accounts, three savings accounts, and an additional checking account totaling $4,000. You will be well on your way to rebuilding your credit.

Note: Some banks may not loan you the full $1,000. They may limit you to 75% of the deposit that you have with them. Don't let that discourage you.

Let's recap what you did. You initially deposited $1,000 and took out a loan for $1,000 for a term of one year. You then repeated the process two more times. You now have three banks reporting your loans to the credit bureau.

The next step is to apply for department store cards. Once you receive the cards go on a shopping spree and charge close to the max. I hear you gasping already. But, before you get too excited about spending again, you have one more step in this process. About a week later you return everything unopened. The result of this method will be that the department store will have you on record as maxing out and paying in full. Make sure you know the return policy of each store before doing this.

It's important to note that these methods take discipline. If you get out of control again you could end up worse than you were before. Credit is a double-edged sword. Used the right way you can make yourself a financial powerhouse.

Treat your credit cards as cash. Keep the credit cards only for medical, job loss, emergencies, or unexpected expenses (such as car repairs).

Chapter Eleven

Sample Letters to Creditors and Credit Bureaus

The following is a sample letter requesting the removal of inaccurate information.

Your Name
Your street Address
Your City, St, Zip Code

Name of Credit Bureau
Bureau's Address
City, St, Zip Code

Date

Dear Credit Bureau,

This letter is a formal complaint that you are reporting inaccurate information on my credit report.

I am very bothered that you have included the below information in my credit report due to its negative effects on my good credit standing. The Federal Fair Credit Reporting Act ensures that only accurate information be reported on my credit report. Obviously, due to a mistake by either you or the creditor, this misinformation is appearing on my credit report. Because of this negative information appearing on my credit report I was recently denied credit for a (insert here what type of credit you were denied for).

Enclosed is proof to contradict the negative information being reported about me. I trust you will investigate this claim and remove this ASAP.

Please verify the following information and delete it from my report as soon as possible.
XYC Finance, Acct# 123-3458

Sincerely,
Your Name

Sample letter two

To Whom It May Concern:

Your Name
SSN 123-45-6789
Address
(Additional address for last five years)
DOB 1/1/00

I have just reviewed my credit report and have noticed several inaccurate items on my report:

XYZ Finance Acct # 123-4567:

This account is being listed as being 30 days late. I have never been late on this account.

ABC Furniture Mart Acct# 999-0999
This account is being listed as being 30 days late. I have never been late on this account.

In addition, there are two accounts that have been inactive for more than seven years. The FCRA states that all credit information older than seven years should be removed from my report. The following accounts should be removed:

Nationsbank Acct#12345
GTE Visa Acct#1234567

I have enclosed a copy of my driver's license and social security card as proof of my identity.

Sincerely,

Your Name

The following is a sample letter you can use to remove unauthorized inquiries into your credit report:

Your Name
Your Street Address
Your City, State, Zip Code

Name of Creditor
Creditor's Address
City, State, Zip Code

Dear Creditor,

I recently received a copy of my credit report from Equifax and noticed there was an inquiry from your company. I did not authorize your company to inquire into my credit. Please have the inquiry removed from my credit report as it is making it difficult for me to obtain credit.

I need your prompt attention to this matter. As a result I have sent this letter Certified mail. Please forward documentation showing the unauthorized inquiry has been removed from my credit report.

If you find that I am wrong in my claim, please forward any supporting documentation you have that shows I authorized this inquiry.

Thank You,

Your Name

Sample letter for "No response to a dispute letter"

Date _________

From: Your Name

To: Customer Relations
Credit Reporting Agency
Address
City, State, Zip

Subject: No Response From Your Office

On (date) I requested an investigation of certain items contained in my credit file. Enclosed is a copy of that letter.

The Fair Credit Reporting Act states a response is required from you within 30 days. As you can see from the date of the letter we are well past the 30 days allowed. I assume you have not responded because the disputed items cannot be verified. Therefore, please delete these items and send me a corrected copy of my credit file.

Thank you,

Signature
Your Name
SSN
Address
City, State, Zip
Date of Birth
Phone Number (optional)

Sample letter to follow up previous letter

Date

From: Your Name
To: Customer Relations
Credit Reporting Agency
Address
City, State, Zip

Subject: Continued Response From Your Office

On (date) I requested a reinvestigation of certain items contained in my credit file. Additionally, on (date), I made a second request. Enclosed is a copy of both letters.

The Fair Credit Reporting Act specifically states a prompt response. This has not happened. I assume you have not responded because the disputed items cannot be verified. Therefore, please delete these items and send me a corrected copy of my credit file.

Please note that a copy of this letter is being forwarded to the Federal Trade Commission for compliance.

Thank you,

Signature
Name
SSN
Address
City, State, Zip
Date of Birth
Phone Number (optional)
CC: Federal Trade Commission

Dispute Re-Examination Findings

Date

From: Your Name

To: Customer Relations
Credit Reporting Agency
Address
City, State, Zip

Subject: Dispute Investigation Findings

I disagree with the findings of your investigation concerning the following items:

____.

Please re-investigate and provide me with the company names and addresses of those merchants with whom you verified the information so that I may contact them myself. Please forward this information to me as well as an updated copy of my credit file.

(The following statement is optional) I do not wish to include my disagreement with your re-investigation as part of my 100-word statement to my credit file at this time.

Thank you,

Signature
Your Name
SSN
Address
City, State, Zip
Date of Birth
Phone Number (optional)

Here is a sample letter that you can use once a settlement has been reached. If possible hand-deliver the letter, be careful about a return address if you have to mail it.

Date

Name of Creditor
Address
RE: Account

ATT:

The purpose of this letter is to confirm our previous telephone conversation on ____________ (date) regarding the settlement of the above account. According to our verbal agreement on the telephone, I will pay your company the amount of $________________ as full settlement of this account. Also, according to our verbal agreement, upon receipt of the above consideration, your company has agreed to change the remark on my credit file to "paid satisfactorily". In addition, any reference to any late payment or charge-off regarding this account will be deleted from my credit file. The updated status will then be reported to all credit bureaus that you report to.

Your cooperation in this matter is greatly appreciated. If this settlement agreement is acceptable to your company, please acknowledge with your signature in the space provided below and return a copy to me. Upon, receipt of this signed acknowledgement, I will forward you the amount stated above.

____ ______

(Signature of authorized officer) (Date)

Thank you,

Your Name

OPT-OUT

To opt-out of the release of your name for marketing purposes contact:

The three major credit bureaus offer the following number for opting-out of all pre-approved credit offers: 1-888-567-8688.

Or write:

Equifax, Inc.
Options
PO Box 740123
Atlanta, GA 30374-0123

Experian
Consumer Opt-Out
701 Experian Parkway
Allen, TX 75013

Trans Union
Marketing List Opt Out
PO Box 97328
Jackson, MS 39288-7328

See sample of an opt-out letter on the following page.

Sample letter to opt-out

To Whom It May Concern:

I request to have my name removed from your marketing lists. Here is the information you have asked me to include in my request:

FIRST, MIDDLE, LAST NAME

____

(List all name variations, including Jr., Sr., etc.)

CURRENT MAILING LIST

____

____

____

PREVIOUS MAILING LIST

____

(fill in your previous mailing address if you
have moved in the last 6 months.)
Note: not required by Equifax and Experian.

____

____

____

Social Security Number

____

Note: Not required by Experian

Date of Birth

____

Note: Not required by Equifax and Experian.

Thank you for your prompt handling of my request.

____

Signature

The Direct Marketing Association (DMA) offers the Mail and Telephone Preference Services (TPS), which allow you to opt-out of direct mail marketing and/or telemarketing from many national companies.

Registering with DMA will reduce the amount of unsolicited national advertising mail and telemarketing you receive. Registering with DMA is a free service.

DMA does not provide marketers with consumer mailing lists or telephone numbers. The Mail Preference Service and the Telephone Preference Service are available to companies for the sole purpose of removing your name and home address from their mailing lists. Your information remains on file for 5 years. This service does not apply to advertising mail sent to your business address.

After several months you will begin receiving less advertising mail and telemarketing phone calls from national marketers such as credit cards, sweepstakes and magazine subscription offers, and catalogs. Local businesses and organizations usually do not use this program. You will continue to receive mail and/or phone calls from companies with which you already do business.

Not all companies use MPS or TPS to purge their mailing lists, therefore, you may continue to receive some companies' promotions. In this instance, contact the company directly and ask to be placed on the company's do-not-mail file.

To opt-out, simply write one letter with the statement PLEASE REGISTER MY NAME WITH THE MAIL PREFERENCE SERVICE and one letter with PLEASE REGISTER MY NAME WITH TELEPHONE PREFERENCE SERVICE

Include your name, street address, city, state, and zip code. Include your telephone number when mailing to the TPS. Don't forget to sign your name at the bottom of each letter.

Mail to:

Direct Marketing Association
Mail Preference Service
PO Box 9008
Farmingdale, NY 11735-9008

Direct Marketing Association
Telephone Preference Service
PO Box 9014
Farmingdale, NY 11735-9014

Appendix

The Fair Credit Reporting Act

As a public service, the staff of the Federal Trade Commission (FTC) has prepared the following complete text of the Fair Credit Reporting Act (FCRA), 15 U.S.C. § 1681 et seq. Although staff generally followed the format of the U.S. Code as published by the Government Printing Office, the format of this text does differ in minor ways from the Code (and from West's U.S. Code Annotated). For example, this version uses FCRA section numbers (§§ 601-625) in the headings. (The relevant U.S. Code citation is included with each section heading and each reference to the FCRA in the text.)

This version of the FCRA is complete as of November 27, 1998. It includes the amendments to the FCRA set forth in the Consumer Credit Reporting Reform Act of 1996 (Public Law 104-208, the Omnibus Consolidated Appropriations Act for Fiscal Year 1997, Title II, Subtitle D, Chapter 1), Section 311 of the Intelligence Authorization for Fiscal Year 1998 (Public Law 105-107), and the Consumer Reporting Employment Clarification Act of 1998 (Public Law 105-347).

Table of Contents

§ 601. Short title

This title may be cited as the Fair Credit Reporting Act.

§ 602. Congressional findings and statement of purpose [15 U.S.C. § 1681]

(a) Accuracy and fairness of credit reporting. The Congress makes the following findings:

(1) The banking system is dependent upon fair and accurate credit reporting. Inaccurate credit reports directly impair the efficiency of the banking system, and unfair credit reporting methods undermine the public confidence which is essential to the continued functioning of the banking system.

(2) An elaborate mechanism has been developed for investigating and evaluating the credit worthiness, credit standing, credit capacity, character, and general reputation of consumers.

(3) Consumer reporting agencies have assumed a vital role in assembling and evaluating consumer credit and other information on consumers.

(4) There is a need to insure that consumer reporting agencies exercise their grave responsibilities with fairness, impartiality, and a respect for the consumer's right to privacy.

(b) Reasonable procedures. It is the purpose of this title to require that consumer reporting agencies adopt reasonable procedures for meeting the needs of commerce for consumer credit, personnel, insurance, and other information in a manner which is fair and equitable to the consumer, with regard to the confidentiality, accuracy, relevancy, and proper utilization of such information in accordance with the requirements of this title.

§ 603. Definitions; rules of construction [15 U.S.C. § 1681a]

(a) Definitions and rules of construction set forth in this section are applicable for the purposes of this title.

(b) The term "person" means any individual, partnership, corporation, trust, estate, cooperative, association, government or governmental subdivision or agency, or other entity.

(c) The term "consumer" means an individual.

(d) Consumer report.

(1) In general. The term "consumer report" means any written, oral, or other communication of any information by a consumer reporting agency bearing on a consumer's credit worthiness, credit standing, credit capacity, character, general reputation, personal characteristics, or mode of living which is used or expected to be used or collected in whole or in part for the purpose of serving as a factor in establishing the consumer's eligibility for

(A) credit or insurance to be used primarily for personal, family, or household purposes;

(B) employment purposes; or

(C) any other purpose authorized under section 604 [§ 1681b].

(2) Exclusions. The term "consumer report" does not include

(A) any

(i) report containing information solely as to transactions or experiences between the consumer and the person making the report;

(ii) communication of that information among persons related by common ownership or affiliated by corporate control; or

(iii) communication of other information among persons related by common ownership or affiliated by corporate control, if it is clearly and conspicuously disclosed to the consumer that the information may be communicated among such persons and the consumer is given the opportunity, before the time that the information is initially communicated, to direct that such information not be communicated among such persons;

(B) any authorization or approval of a specific extension of credit directly or indirectly by the issuer of a credit card or similar device;

(C) any report in which a person who has been requested by a third party to make a specific extension of credit directly or indirectly to a consumer conveys his or her decision with response to such request, if the third party advises the consumer of the name and address of the person to whom the request was made, and such person makes the disclosures to the consumer required under section 615 [§ 1681m]; or

(D) a communication described in subsection (o).

(e) The term "investigative consumer report" means a consumer report or portion thereof in which information on a consumer's character, general reputation, personal characteristics, or mode of living is obtained

through personal interviews with neighbors, friends, or associates of the consumer reported on or with others with whom he is acquainted or who may have knowledge concerning any such items of information. However, such information shall not include specific factual information on a consumer's credit record obtained directly from a creditor of the consumer or from a consumer reporting agency when such information was obtained directly from a creditor of the consumer or from the consumer.

(f) The term "consumer reporting agency" means any person which, for monetary fees, dues, or on a cooperative nonprofit basis, regularly engages in whole or in part in the practice of assembling or evaluating consumer credit information or other information on consumers for the purpose of furnishing consumer reports to third parties, and which uses any means or facility of interstate commerce for the purpose of preparing or furnishing consumer reports.

(g) The term "file," when used in connection with information on any consumer, means all of the information on that consumer recorded and retained by a consumer reporting agency regardless of how the information is stored.

(h) The term "employment purposes" when used in connection with a consumer report means a report used for the purpose of evaluating a consumer for employment, promotion, reassignment or retention as an employee.

(i) The term "medical information" means information or records obtained, with the consent of the individual to whom it relates, from licensed physicians or medical practitioners, hospitals, clinics, or other medical or medically related facilities.

(j) Definitions relating to child support obligations.

(1) Overdue support. The term "overdue support" has the meaning given to such term in section 666(e) of title 42 [Social Security Act, 42 U.S.C. § 666(e)].

(2) State or local child support enforcement agency. The term "State or local child support enforcement agency" means a State or local agency which administers a State or local program for establishing and enforcing child support obligations.

(k) Adverse action.

(1) Actions included. The term "adverse action"

(A) has the same meaning as in section 701(d)(6) of the Equal Credit Opportunity Act; and

(B) means

(i) a denial or cancellation of, an increase in any charge for, or a reduction or other adverse or unfavorable change in the terms of coverage or amount of, any insurance, existing or applied for, in connection with the underwriting of insurance;

(ii) a denial of employment or any other decision for employment purposes that adversely affects any current or prospective employee;

(iii) a denial or cancellation of, an increase in any charge for, or any other adverse or unfavorable change in the terms of, any license or benefit described in section 604(a)(3)(D) [§ 1681b]; and

(iv) an action taken or determination that is

(I) made in connection with an application that was made by, or a transaction that was initiated by, any consumer, or in connection with a review of an account under section 604(a)(3)(F)(ii)[§ 1681b]; and

(II) adverse to the interests of the consumer.

(2) Applicable findings, decisions, commentary, and orders. For purpose of any determination of whether an action is an adverse action under paragraph (1)(A), all appropriate final findings, decisions, commentary, and orders issued under section 701(d)(6) of the Equal Credit Opportunity Act by the Board of Governors of the Federal Reserve System or any court shall apply.

(l) Firm offer of credit or insurance. The term "firm offer of credit or insurance" means any offer of credit or insurance to a consumer that will be honored if the consumer is determined, based on information in a consumer report on the consumer, to meet the specific criteria used to select the consumer for the offer, except that the offer may be further conditioned on one or more of the following:

(1) The consumer being determined, based on information in the consumer's application for the credit or insurance, to meet specific criteria bearing on credit worthiness or insurability, as applicable, that are established

(A) before selection of the consumer for the offer; and

(B) for the purpose of determining whether to extend credit or insurance pursuant to the offer.

(2) Verification

(A) that the consumer continues to meet the specific criteria used to select the consumer for the offer, by using information in a consumer report on the consumer, information in the consumer's application for the credit or insurance, or other information bearing on the credit worthiness or insurability of the consumer; or

(B) of the information in the consumer's application for the credit or insurance, to determine that the consumer meets the specific criteria bearing on credit worthiness or insurability.

(3) The consumer furnishing any collateral that is a requirement for the extension of

the credit or insurance that was

(A) established before selection of the consumer for the offer of credit or insurance; and

(B) disclosed to the consumer in the offer of credit or insurance.

(m) Credit or insurance transaction that is not initiated by the consumer.

The term "credit or insurance transaction that is not initiated by the consumer" does not include the use of a consumer report by a person with which the consumer has an account or insurance policy, for purposes of

(1) reviewing the account or insurance policy; or

(2) collecting the account.

(n) State. The term "State" means any State, the Commonwealth of Puerto Rico, the District of Columbia, and any territory or possession of the United States.

(o) Excluded communications. A communication is described in this subsection if it is a communication

(1) that, but for subsection (d)(2)(D), would be an investigative consumer report;

(2) that is made to a prospective employer for the purpose of

(A) procuring an employee for the employer; or

(B) procuring an opportunity for a natural person to work for the employer;

(3) that is made by a person who regularly performs such procurement;

(4) that is not used by any person for any purpose other than a purpose described in subparagraph (A) or (B) of paragraph (2); and

(5) with respect to which

(A) the consumer who is the subject of the communication

(i) consents orally or in writing to the nature and scope of the communication, before the collection of any information for the purpose of making the communication;

(ii) consents orally or in writing to the making of the communication to a prospective employer, before the making of the communication; and

(iii) in the case of consent under clause (i) or (ii) given orally, is provided written confirmation of that consent by the person making the communication, not later than 3 business days after the receipt of the consent by that person;

(B) the person who makes the communication does not, for the purpose of making the communication, make any inquiry that if made by a prospective employer of the consumer who is the subject of the communication would violate any applicable Federal or State equal

employment opportunity law or regulation; and

(C) the person who makes the communication

(i) discloses in writing to the consumer who is the subject of the communication, not later than 5 business days after receiving any request from the consumer for such disclosure, the nature and substance of all information in the consumer's file at the time of the request, except that the sources of any information that is acquired solely for use in making the communication and is actually used for no other purpose, need not be disclosed other than under appropriate discovery procedures in any court of competent jurisdiction in which an action is brought; and

(ii) notifies the consumer who is the subject of the communication,in writing, of the consumer's right to request the information described in clause (i).

(p) Consumer reporting agency that compiles and maintains files on consumers on a nationwide basis. The term "consumer reporting agency that compiles and maintains files on consumers on a nationwide basis" means a consumer reporting agency that regularly engages in the practice of assembling or evaluating, and maintaining, for the purpose of furnishing consumer reports to third parties bearing on a consumer's credit worthiness, credit standing, or credit capacity, each of the following regarding consumers residing nationwide:

(1) Public record information.

(2) Credit account information from persons who furnish that information regularly and in the ordinary course of business.

§ 604. Permissible purposes of consumer reports [15 U.S.C. § 1681b]

(a) In general. Subject to subsection (c), any consumer reporting agency may furnish a consumer report under the following circumstances and no other:

(1) In response to the order of a court having jurisdiction to issue such an order, or a subpoena issued in connection with proceedings before a Federal grand jury.

(2) In accordance with the written instructions of the consumer to whom it relates.

(3) To a person which it has reason to believe

(A) intends to use the information in connection with a credit transaction involving the consumer on whom the information is to be furnished and involving the extension of credit to, or review or collection of an account of, the consumer; or

(B) intends to use the information for employment purposes; or

(C) intends to use the information in connection with the underwriting of insurance

involving the consumer; or

(D) intends to use the information in connection with a determination of the consumer's eligibility for a license or other benefit granted by a governmental instrumentality required by law to consider an applicant's financial responsibility or status; or

(E) intends to use the information, as a potential investor or servicer, or current insurer, in connection with a valuation of, or an assessment of the credit or prepayment risks associated with, an existing credit obligation; or

(F) otherwise has a legitimate business need for the information

(i) in connection with a business transaction that is initiated by the consumer; or

(ii) to review an account to determine whether the consumer continues to meet the terms of the account.

(4) In response to a request by the head of a State or local child support enforcement agency (or a State or local government official authorized by the head of such an agency), if the person making the request certifies to the consumer reporting agency that

(A) the consumer report is needed for the purpose of establishing an individual's capacity to make child support payments or determining the appropriate level of such payments;

(B) the paternity of the consumer for the child to which the obligation relates has been established or acknowledged by the consumer in accordance with State laws under which the obligation arises (if required by those laws);

(C) the person has provided at least 10 days' prior notice to the consumer whose report is requested, by certified or registered mail to the last known address of the consumer, that the report will be requested; and

(D) the consumer report will be kept confidential, will be used solely for a purpose described in subparagraph (A), and will not be used in connection with any other civil, administrative, or criminal proceeding, or for any other purpose.

(5) To an agency administering a State plan under Section 454 of the Social Security Act (42 U.S.C. § 654) for use to set an initial or modified child support award.

(b) Conditions for furnishing and using consumer reports for employment purposes.

(1) Certification from user. A consumer reporting agency may furnish a consumer report for employment purposes only if

(A) the person who obtains such report from the agency certifies to the agency that

(i) the person has complied with paragraph (2) with respect to the consumer report, and the person will comply with paragraph (3) with respect to the consumer report if paragraph (3) becomes applicable; and

(ii) information from the consumer report will not be used in violation of any applicable Federal or State equal employment opportunity law or regulation; and

(B) the consumer reporting agency provides with the report, or has previously provided, a summary of the consumer's rights under this title, as prescribed by the Federal Trade Commission under section 609(c)(3) [§ 1681g].

(2) Disclosure to consumer.

(A) In general. Except as provided in subparagraph (B), a person may not procure a consumer report, or cause a consumer report to be procured, for employment purposes with respect to any consumer, unless—

(i) a clear and conspicuous disclosure has been made in writing to the consumer at any time before the report is procured or caused to be procured, in a document that consists solely of the disclosure, that a consumer report may be obtained for employment purposes; and

(ii) the consumer has authorized in writing (which authorization may be made on the document referred to in clause (i)) the procurement of the report by that person.

(B) Application by mail, telephone, computer, or other similar means. If a consumer described in subparagraph (C) applies for employment by mail, telephone, computer, or other similar means, at any time before a consumer report is procured or caused to be procured in connection with that application—

(i) the person who procures the consumer report on the consumer for employment purposes shall provide to the consumer, by oral, written, or electronic means, notice that a consumer report may be obtained for employment purposes, and a summary of the consumer's rights under section 615(a)(3); and

(ii) the consumer shall have consented, orally, in writing, or electronically to the procurement of the report by that person.

(C) Scope. Subparagraph (B) shall apply to a person procuring a consumer report on a consumer in connection with the consumer's application for employment only if—

(i) the consumer is applying for a position over which the Secretary of Transportation has the power to establish qualifications and maximum hours of service pursuant to the provisions of section 31502 of title 49, or a position subject to safety regulation by a State transportation agency; and

(ii) as of the time at which the person procures the report or causes the report to be procured the only interaction between the consumer and the person in connection with that employment application has been by mail, telephone, computer, or other similar means.

(3) Conditions on use for adverse actions.

(A) In general. Except as provided in subparagraph (B), in using a consumer report for employment purposes, before taking any adverse action based in whole or in part on the report, the person intending to take such adverse action shall provide to the consumer to whom the report relates—

(i) a copy of the report; and

(ii) a description in writing of the rights of the consumer under this title, as prescribed by the Federal Trade Commission under section 609(c)(3).

(B) Application by mail, telephone, computer, or other similar means.

(i) If a consumer described in subparagraph (C) applies for employment by mail, telephone, computer, or other similar means, and if a person who has procured a consumer report on the consumer for employment purposes takes adverse action on the employment application based in whole or in part on the report, then the person must provide to the consumer to whom the report relates, in lieu of the notices required under subparagraph (A) of this section and under section 615(a), within 3 business days of taking such action, an oral, written or electronic notification—

(I) that adverse action has been taken based in whole or in part on a consumer report received from a consumer reporting agency;

(II) of the name, address and telephone number of the consumer reporting agency that furnished the consumer report (including a toll-free telephone number established by the agency if the agency compiles and maintains files on consumers on a nationwide basis);

(III) that the consumer reporting agency did not make the decision to take the adverse action and is unable to provide to the consumer the specific reasons why the adverse action was taken; and

(IV) that the consumer may, upon providing proper identification, request a free copy of a report and may dispute with the consumer reporting agency the accuracy or completeness of any information in a report.

(ii) If, under clause (B)(i)(IV), the consumer requests a copy of a consumer report from the person who procured the report, then, within 3 business days of receiving the consumer's request, together with proper identification, the person must send or provide to the consumer a copy of a report and a copy of the consumer's rights as prescribed by the Federal Trade Commission under section 609(c)(3).

(C) Scope. Subparagraph (B) shall apply to a person procuring a consumer report on a consumer in connection with the consumer's application for employment only if—

(i) the consumer is applying for a position over which the Secretary of Transportation has the power to establish qualifications and maximum hours of service pursuant to the provisions of section 31502 of title 49, or a position subject to safety regulation by a State transportation agency; and

(ii) as of the time at which the person procures the report or causes the report to be procured the only interaction between the consumer and the person in connection with that employment application has been by mail, telephone, computer, or other similar means.

(4) Exception for national security investigations.

(A) In general. In the case of an agency or department of the United States Government which seeks to obtain and use a consumer report for employment purposes, paragraph (3) shall not apply to any adverse action by such agency or department which is based in part on such consumer report, if the head of such agency or department makes a written finding that—

(i) the consumer report is relevant to a national security investigation of such agency or department;

(ii) the investigation is within the jurisdiction of such agency or department;

(iii) there is reason to believe that compliance with paragraph (3) will—

(I) endanger the life or physical safety of any person;

(II) result in flight from prosecution;

(III) result in the destruction of, or tampering with, evidence relevant to the investigation;

(IV) result in the intimidation of a potential witness relevant to the investigation;

(V) result in the compromise of classified information; or

(VI) otherwise seriously jeopardize or unduly delay the investigation or another official proceeding.

(B) Notification of consumer upon conclusion of investigation. Upon the conclusion of a national security investigation described in subparagraph (A), or upon the determination that the exception under subparagraph (A) is no longer required for the reasons set forth in such subparagraph, the official exercising the authority in such subparagraph shall provide to the consumer who is the subject of the consumer report with regard to which such finding was made—

(i) a copy of such consumer report with any classified information redacted as necessary;

(ii) notice of any adverse action which is based, in part, on the consumer report; and

(iii) the identification with reasonable specificity of the nature of the investigation for which the consumer report was sought.

(C) Delegation by head of agency or department. For purposes of

subparagraphs (A) and (B), the head of any agency or department of the United States Government may delegate his or her authorities under this paragraph to an official of such agency or department who has

personnel security responsibilities and is a member of the Senior Executive Service or equivalent civilian or military rank.

(D) Report to the congress. Not later than January 31 of each year, the head of each agency and department of the United States Government that exercised authority under this paragraph during the preceding year shall submit a report to the Congress on the number of times the department or agency exercised such authority during the year.

(E) Definitions. For purposes of this paragraph, the following definitions shall apply:

(i) Classified information. The term 'classified information' means information that is protected from unauthorized disclosure under Executive Order No. 12958 or successor orders.

(c) Furnishing reports in connection with credit or insurance transactions that are not initiated by the consumer.

(1) In general. A consumer reporting agency may furnish a consumer report relating to any consumer pursuant to subparagraph (A) or (C) of subsection (a)(3) in connection with any credit or insurance transaction that is not initiated by the consumer only if

(A) the consumer authorizes the agency to provide such report to such person; or

(B) (i) the transaction consists of a firm offer of credit or insurance;

(ii) the consumer reporting agency has complied with subsection (e); and

(iii) there is not in effect an election by the consumer, made in accordance with subsection (e), to have the consumer's name and address excluded from lists of names provided by the agency pursuant to this paragraph.

(2) Limits on information received under paragraph (1)(B). A person may receive pursuant to paragraph (1)(B) only

(A) the name and address of a consumer;

(B) an identifier that is not unique to the consumer and that is used by the person solely for the purpose of verifying the identity of the consumer; and

(C) other information pertaining to a consumer that does not identify the relationship or experience of the consumer with respect to a particular creditor or other entity.

(3) Information regarding inquiries. Except as provided in section 609(a)(5) [§ 1681g], a consumer reporting agency shall not furnish to any person a record of inquiries in connection with a credit or insurance transaction that is not initiated by a consumer.

(d) Reserved.

(e) Election of consumer to be excluded from lists.

(1) In general. A consumer may elect to have the consumer's name and address excluded from any list provided by a consumer reporting agency under subsection (c)(1)(B) in connection with a credit or insurance transaction that is not initiated by the consumer, by notifying the agency in accordance with paragraph (2) that the consumer does not consent to any use of a consumer report relating to the consumer in connection with any credit or insurance transaction that is not initiated by the consumer.

(2) Manner of notification. A consumer shall notify a consumer reporting agency under paragraph (1)

(A) through the notification system maintained by the agency under paragraph (5); or

(B) by submitting to the agency a signed notice of election form issued by the agency for purposes of this subparagraph.

(3) Response of agency after notification through system. Upon receipt of notification of the election of a consumer under paragraph (1) through the notification system maintained by the agency under paragraph (5), a consumer reporting agency shall

(A) inform the consumer that the election is effective only for the 2-year period following the election if the consumer does not submit to the agency a signed notice of election form issued by the agency for purposes of paragraph (2)(B); and

(B) provide to the consumer a notice of election form, if requested by the consumer, not later than 5 business days after receipt of the notification of the election through the system established under paragraph (5), in the case of a request made at the time the consumer provides notification through the system.

(4) Effectiveness of election. An election of a consumer under paragraph

(1)

(A) shall be effective with respect to a consumer reporting agency beginning 5 business days after the date on which the consumer notifies the agency in accordance with paragraph (2);

(B) shall be effective with respect to a consumer reporting agency

(i) subject to subparagraph (C), during the 2-year period beginning 5 business days after the date on which the consumer notifies the agency of the election, in the case of an election for which a consumer notifies the agency only in accordance with paragraph (2)(A); or

(ii) until the consumer notifies the agency under subparagraph (C), in the case of an election for which a consumer notifies the agency in accordance with paragraph (2)(B);

(C) shall not be effective after the date on which the consumer notifies the agency, through the notification system established by the agency under paragraph (5), that the election is no longer effective; and

(D) shall be effective with respect to each affiliate of the agency.

(5) Notification system.

(A) In general. Each consumer reporting agency that, under subsection (c)(1)(B), furnishes a consumer report in connection with a credit or insurance transaction that is not initiated by a consumer, shall

(i) establish and maintain a notification system, including a toll-free telephone number, which permits any consumer whose consumer report is maintained by the agency to notify the agency, with appropriate identification, of the consumer's election to have the consumer's name and address excluded from any such list of names and addresses provided by the agency for such a transaction; and

(ii) publish by not later than 365 days after the date of enactment of the Consumer Credit Reporting Reform Act of 1996, and not less than annually thereafter, in a publication of general circulation in the area served by the agency

(I) a notification that information in consumer files maintained by the agency may be used in connection with such transactions; and

(II) the address and toll-free telephone number for consumers to use to notify the agency of the consumer's election under clause (I).

(B) Establishment and maintenance as compliance. Establishment and

maintenance of a notification system (including a toll-free telephone number) and publication by a consumer reporting agency on the agency's own behalf and on behalf of any of its affiliates in accordance with this paragraph is deemed to be compliance with this paragraph by each of those affiliates.

(6) Notification system by agencies that operate nationwide. Each consumer reporting agency that compiles and maintains files on consumers on a nationwide basis shall establish and maintain a notification system for purposes of paragraph (5) jointly with other such consumer reporting agencies.

(f) Certain use or obtaining of information prohibited. A person shall not use or obtain a consumer report for any purpose unless

(1) the consumer report is obtained for a purpose for which the consumer report is authorized to be furnished under this section; and

(2) the purpose is certified in accordance with section 607 [§ 1681e] by a prospective user of the report through a general or specific certification.

(g) Furnishing reports containing medical information. A consumer reporting agency shall not furnish for employment purposes, or in connection with a credit or insurance transaction, a consumer report that contains medical information about a consumer, unless the consumer consents to the furnishing of the report.

§ 605. Requirements relating to information contained in consumer reports [15 U.S.C. § 1681c]

(a) Information excluded from consumer reports. Except as authorized under subsection (b) of this section, no consumer reporting agency may make any consumer report containing any of the following items of information:

(1) Cases under title 11 [United States Code] or under the Bankruptcy Act that, from the date of entry of the order for relief or the date of

adjudication, as the case may be, antedate the report by more than 10 years.

(2) Civil suits, civil judgments, and records of arrest that from date of entry, antedate the report by more than seven years or until the governing statute of limitations has expired, whichever is the longer period.

(3) Paid tax liens which, from date of payment, antedate the report by more than seven years.

(4) Accounts placed for collection or charged to profit and loss which antedate the report by more than seven years.(1)

(5) Any other adverse item of information, other than records of

convictions of crimes which antedates the report by more than seven years.1

(b) Exempted cases. The provisions of subsection (a) of this section are not applicable in the case of any consumer credit report to be used in connection with

(1) a credit transaction involving, or which may reasonably be expected to involve, a principal amount of $150,000 or more;

(2) the underwriting of life insurance involving, or which may reasonably be expected to involve, a face amount of $150,000 or more; or

(3) the employment of any individual at an annual salary which equals, or which may reasonably be expected to equal $75,000, or more.

(c) Running of reporting period.

(1) In general. The 7-year period referred to in paragraphs (4) and (6) of subsection (a) shall begin, with respect to any delinquent account that is placed for collection (internally or by referral to a third party, whichever is earlier), charged to profit and loss, or subjected to any similar action, upon the expiration of the 180-day period beginning on the date of the commencement of the delinquency which immediately preceded the collection activity, charge to profit and loss, or similar action.

(2) Effective date. Paragraph (1) shall apply only to items of information added to the file of a consumer on or after the date that is 455 days after the date of enactment of the Consumer Credit Reporting Reform Act of 1996.

(d) Information required to be disclosed. Any consumer reporting agency that furnishes a consumer report that contains information regarding any case involving the consumer that arises under title 11, United States Code, shall include in the report an identification of the chapter of such title 11 under which such case arises if provided by the source of the information. If any case arising or filed under title 11, United States Code, is withdrawn by the consumer before a final judgment, the consumer reporting agency shall include in the report that such case or filing was withdrawn upon receipt of documentation certifying such withdrawal.

(e) Indication of closure of account by consumer. If a consumer reporting agency is notified pursuant to section 623(a)(4) [§ 1681s-2] that a credit account of a consumer was voluntarily closed by the consumer, the agency shall indicate that fact in any consumer report that includes information related to the account.

(f) Indication of dispute by consumer. If a consumer reporting agency is notified pursuant to section 623(a)(3) [§ 1681s-2] that information regarding a consumer who was furnished to the agency is disputed by the consumer, the agency shall indicate that fact in each consumer report that includes the disputed information.

§ 606. Disclosure of investigative consumer reports [15 U.S.C. § 1681d]

(a) Disclosure of fact of preparation. A person may not procure or cause to be prepared an investigative consumer report on any consumer unless

(1) it is clearly and accurately disclosed to the consumer that an investigative consumer report including information as to his character, general reputation, personal characteristics and mode of living, whichever are applicable, may be made, and such disclosure

(A) is made in a writing mailed, or otherwise delivered, to the consumer, not later than three days after the date on which the report was first requested, and

(B) includes a statement informing the consumer of his right to request the additional disclosures provided for under subsection (b) of this section and the written summary of the rights of the consumer prepared pursuant to section 609(c) [§ 1681g]; and

(2) the person certifies or has certified to the consumer reporting agency that

(A) the person has made the disclosures to the consumer required by paragraph (1); and

(B) the person will comply with subsection (b).

(b) Disclosure on request of nature and scope of investigation. Any person who procures or causes to be prepared an investigative consumer report on any consumer shall, upon written request made by the consumer within a reasonable period of time after the receipt by him of the disclosure required by subsection (a)(1) of this section, make a complete and accurate disclosure of the nature and scope of the investigation requested. This disclosure shall be made in a writing mailed, or otherwise delivered, to the consumer not later than five days after the date on which the request for such disclosure was received from the consumer or such report was first requested, whichever is the later.

(c) Limitation on liability upon showing of reasonable procedures for compliance with provisions. No person may be held liable for any violation of subsection (a) or (b) of this section if he shows by a preponderance of the evidence that at the time of the violation he maintained reasonable procedures to assure compliance with subsection (a) or (b) of this section.

(d) Prohibitions.

(1) Certification. A consumer reporting agency shall not prepare or furnish investigative consumer report unless the agency has received a certification under subsection (a)(2) from the person who requested the report.

(2) Inquiries. A consumer reporting agency shall not make an inquiry for the purpose of preparing an investigative consumer report on a consumer for employment purposes if the making of the inquiry by an employer or prospective employer of the consumer would violate any applicable Federal or State equal employment opportunity law or regulation.

(3) Certain public record information. Except as otherwise provided in section 613 [§ 1681k], a consumer reporting agency shall not furnish an investigative consumer report that includes information that is a matter of public record and that relates to an arrest, indictment, conviction, civil judicial action, tax lien, or outstanding judgment, unless the agency has verified the accuracy of the information during the 30-day period ending on the date on which the report is furnished.

(4) Certain adverse information. A consumer reporting agency shall not prepare or furnish an investigative consumer report on a consumer that contains information that is adverse to the interest of the consumer and that is obtained through a personal interview with a neighbor, friend, or associate of the consumer or with another person with whom the consumer is acquainted or who has knowledge of such item of information, unless

(A) the agency has followed reasonable procedures to obtain confirmation of the information, from an additional source that has independent and direct knowledge of the information; or

(B) the person interviewed is the best possible source of the information.

§ 607. Compliance procedures [15 U.S.C. § 1681e]

(a) Identity and purposes of credit users. Every consumer reporting agency shall maintain reasonable procedures designed to avoid violations of section 605 [§ 1681c] and to limit the furnishing of consumer reports to the purposes listed under section 604 [§ 1681b] of this title. These procedures shall require that prospective users of the information identify themselves, certify the purposes for which the information is sought, and certify that the information will be used for no other purpose. Every consumer reporting agency shall make a reasonable effort to verify the identity of a new prospective user and the uses certified by such prospective user prior to furnishing such user a consumer report. No consumer reporting agency may furnish a consumer report to any person if it has reasonable grounds for believing that the consumer report will not be used for a purpose listed in section 604 [§ 1681b] of this title.

(b) Accuracy of report. Whenever a consumer reporting agency prepares a consumer report it shall follow reasonable procedures to assure maximum possible accuracy of the information concerning the individual about whom the report relates.

(c) Disclosure of consumer reports by users allowed. A consumer reporting agency may not prohibit a user of a consumer report furnished by the agency on a consumer from disclosing the contents of the report to the consumer, if adverse action against the consumer has been taken by the user based in whole or in part on the report.

(d) Notice to users and furnishers of information.

(1) Notice requirement. A consumer reporting agency shall provide to any person

(A) who regularly and in the ordinary course of business furnishes information to the agency with respect to any consumer; or

(B) to whom a consumer report is provided by the agency;

a notice of such person's responsibilities under this title.

(2) Content of notice. The Federal Trade Commission shall prescribe the content of notices under paragraph (1), and a consumer reporting agency shall be in compliance with this subsection if it provides a notice under paragraph (1) that is substantially similar to the Federal Trade Commission prescription under this paragraph.

(e) Procurement of consumer report for resale.

(1) Disclosure. A person may not procure a consumer report for purposes of reselling the report (or any information in the report) unless the person discloses to the consumer reporting agency that originally furnishes the report

(A) the identity of the end-user of the report (or information); and

(B) each permissible purpose under section 604 [§ 1681b] for which the report is furnished to the end-user of the report (or information).

(2) Responsibilities of procurers for resale. A person who procures a consumer report for purposes of reselling the report (or any information in the report) shall

(A) establish and comply with reasonable procedures designed to ensure that the report (or information) is resold by the person only for a purpose for which the report may be furnished under section 604 [§ 1681b], including by requiring that each person to which the report (or information) is resold and that resells or provides the report (or information) to any other person

(i) identifies each end user of the resold report (or information);

(ii) certifies each purpose for which the report (or information) will be used; and

(iii) certifies that the report (or information) will be used for no other purpose; and

(B) before reselling the report, make reasonable efforts to verify the identifications and certifications made under subparagraph (A).

§ 608. Disclosures to governmental agencies [15 U.S.C. § 1681f]

Notwithstanding the provisions of section 604 [§ 1681b] of this title, a consumer reporting agency may furnish identifying information respecting any consumer, limited to his name, address, former addresses, places of employment, or former places of employment, to a governmental agency.

§ 609. Disclosures to consumers [15 U.S.C. § 1681g]

(a) Information on file; sources; report recipients. Every consumer reporting agency shall, upon request, and subject to 610(a)(1) [§ 1681h], clearly and accurately disclose to the consumer:

(1) All information in the consumer's file at the time of the request, except that nothing in this paragraph shall be construed to require a consumer reporting agency to disclose to a consumer any information concerning credit scores or any other risk scores or predictors relating to the consumer.

(2) The sources of the information; except that the sources of information acquired solely for use in preparing an investigative consumer report and actually used for no other purpose need not be disclosed: Provided, That in the event an action is brought under this

title, such sources shall be available to the plaintiff under appropriate discovery procedures in the court in which the action is brought.

(3) (A) Identification of each person (including each end-user identified under section 607(e)(1) [§ 1681e]) that procured a consumer report

(i) for employment purposes, during the 2-year period preceding the date on which the request is made; or

(ii) for any other purpose, during the 1-year period preceding the date on which the request is made.

(B) An identification of a person under subparagraph (A) shall include

(i) the name of the person or, if applicable, the trade name (written in full) under which such person conducts business; and

(ii) upon request of the consumer, the address and telephone number of the person.

(C) Subparagraph (A) does not apply if—

(i) the end user is an agency or department of the United States Government that procures the report from the person for purposes of determining the eligibility of the consumer to whom the report relates to receive access or continued access to classified information (as defined in section 604(b)(4)(E)(i)); and

(ii) the head of the agency or department makes a written finding as prescribed under section 604(b)(4)(A).

(4) The dates, original payees, and amounts of any checks upon which is based any adverse characterization of the consumer, included in the file at the time of the disclosure.

(5) A record of all inquiries received by the agency during the 1-year period preceding the request that identified the consumer in connection with a credit or insurance transaction that was not initiated by the consumer.

(b) Exempt information. The requirements of subsection (a) of this section respecting the disclosure of sources of information and the recipients of consumer reports do not apply to information received or consumer reports furnished prior to the effective date of this title except to the extent that the matter involved is contained in the files of the consumer reporting agency on that date.

(c) Summary of rights required to be included with disclosure.

(1) Summary of rights. A consumer reporting agency shall provide to a consumer, with each written disclosure by the agency to the consumer under this section

(A) a written summary of all of the rights that the consumer has under this title; and

(B) in the case of a consumer reporting agency that compiles and maintains files on consumers on a nationwide basis, a toll-free telephone number established by the agency, at which personnel are accessible to consumers during normal business hours.

(2) Specific items required to be included. The summary of rights required under paragraph (1) shall include

(A) a brief description of this title and all rights of consumers under this title;

(B) an explanation of how the consumer may exercise the rights of the consumer under this title;

(C) a list of all Federal agencies responsible for enforcing any provision of this title and the address and any appropriate phone number of each such agency, in a form that will assist the consumer in selecting the appropriate agency;

(D) a statement that the consumer may have additional rights under State law and that the consumer may wish to contact a State or local consumer protection agency or a State attorney general to learn of those rights; and

(E) a statement that a consumer reporting agency is not required to remove accurate derogatory information from a consumer's file, unless the information is outdated under section 605 [§ 1681c] or cannot be verified.

(3) Form of summary of rights. For purposes of this subsection and any disclosure by a consumer reporting agency required under this title with respect to consumers' rights, the Federal Trade Commission (after consultation with each Federal agency referred to in section 621(b) [§ 1681s]) shall prescribe the form and content of any such disclosure of the rights of consumers required under this title. A consumer reporting agency shall be in compliance with this subsection if it provides disclosures under paragraph (1) that are substantially similar to the Federal Trade Commission prescription under this paragraph.

(4) Effectiveness. No disclosures shall be required under this subsection until the date on which the Federal Trade Commission prescribes the form and content of such disclosures under paragraph (3).

§ 610. Conditions and form of disclosure to consumers [15 U.S.C. § 1681h]

(a) In general.

(1) Proper identification. A consumer reporting agency shall require, as a condition of making the disclosures required under section 609 [§ 1681g], that the consumer furnish proper identification.

(2) Disclosure in writing. Except as provided in subsection (b), the disclosures required to be made under section 609 [§ 1681g] shall be provided under that section in writing.

(b) Other forms of disclosure.

(1) In general. If authorized by a consumer, a consumer reporting agency may make the disclosures required under 609 [§ 1681g]

(A) other than in writing; and

(B) in such form as may be

(i) specified by the consumer in accordance with paragraph (2); and

(ii) available from the agency.

(2) Form. A consumer may specify pursuant to paragraph (1) that disclosures under section 609 [§ 1681g] shall be made

(A) in person, upon the appearance of the consumer at the place of business of the consumer reporting agency where disclosures are regularly provided, during normal business hours, and on reasonable notice;

(B) by telephone, if the consumer has made a written request for disclosure by telephone;

(C) by electronic means, if available from the agency; or

(D) by any other reasonable means that is available from the agency.

(c) Trained personnel. Any consumer reporting agency shall provide trained personnel to explain to the consumer any information furnished to him pursuant to section 609 [§ 1681g] of this title.

(d) Persons accompanying consumer. The consumer shall be permitted to be accompanied by one other person of his choosing, who shall furnish reasonable identification. A consumer reporting agency may require the consumer to furnish a written statement granting permission to the consumer reporting agency to discuss the consumer's file in such person's presence.

(e) Limitation of liability. Except as provided in sections 616 and 617 [§§ 1681n and 1681o] of this title, no consumer may bring any action or proceeding in the nature of defamation, invasion of privacy, or negligence with respect to the reporting of information against any consumer reporting agency, any user of information, or any person who furnishes information to a consumer reporting agency, based on information disclosed pursuant to section 609, 610, or 615 [§§ 1681g, 1681h, or 1681m] of this title or based on information disclosed by a user of a consumer report to or for a consumer against whom the user has taken adverse action, based in whole or in part on the report, except as to false information furnished with malice or willful intent to injure such consumer.

§ 611. Procedure in case of disputed accuracy [15 U.S.C. § 1681i]

(a) Reinvestigations of disputed information.

(1) Reinvestigation required.

(A) In general. If the completeness or accuracy of any item of information contained in a consumer's file at a consumer reporting agency is disputed by the consumer and the consumer notifies the agency directly of such dispute, the agency shall reinvestigate free of charge and record the current status of the disputed information, or delete the item from the file in accordance with paragraph (5), before the end of the 30-day period beginning on the date on which the agency receives the notice of the dispute from the consumer.

(B) Extension of period to reinvestigate. Except as provided in subparagraph (C), the 30-day period described in subparagraph (A) may be extended for not more than 15 additional days if the consumer reporting agency receives information from the consumer during that 30-day period that is relevant to the reinvestigation.

(C) Limitations on extension of period to reinvestigate. Subparagraph (B) shall not apply to any reinvestigation in which, during the 30-day period described in subparagraph (A), the information that is the subject of the reinvestigation is found to be inaccurate or incomplete or the consumer reporting agency determines that the information cannot be verified.

(2) Prompt notice of dispute to furnisher of information.

(A) In general. Before the expiration of the 5-business-day period beginning on the date on which a consumer reporting agency receives notice of a dispute from any consumer in accordance with paragraph (1), the agency shall provide notification of the dispute to any person who provided any item of information in dispute, at the address and in the manner established with the person. The notice shall include all relevant information regarding the dispute that the agency has received from the consumer.

(B) Provision of other information from consumer. The consumer reporting agency shall promptly provide to the person who provided the information in dispute all relevant information regarding the dispute that is received by the agency from the consumer after the period referred to in subparagraph (A) and before the end of the period referred to in paragraph (1)(A).

(3) Determination that dispute is frivolous or irrelevant.

(A) In general. Notwithstanding paragraph (1), a consumer reporting agency may terminate a reinvestigation of information disputed by a consumer under that paragraph if the agency reasonably determines that the dispute by the consumer is frivolous or irrelevant, including by reason of a failure by a consumer to provide sufficient information to investigate the disputed information.

(B) Notice of determination. Upon making any determination in accordance with subparagraph (A) that a dispute is frivolous or irrelevant, a consumer reporting agency shall notify the consumer of such determination not later than 5 business days after making such determination, by mail or, if authorized by the consumer for that

purpose, by any other means available to the agency.

(C) Contents of notice. A notice under subparagraph (B) shall include

(i) the reasons for the determination under subparagraph (A); and

(ii) identification of any information required to investigate the disputed information, which may consist of a standardized form describing the general nature of such information.

(4) Consideration of consumer information. In conducting any reinvestigation under paragraph (1) with respect to disputed information in the file of any consumer, the consumer reporting agency shall review and consider all relevant information submitted by the consumer in the period described in paragraph (1)(A) with respect to such disputed information.

(5) Treatment of inaccurate or unverifiable information.

(A) In general. If, after any reinvestigation under paragraph (1) of any information disputed by a consumer, an item of the information is found to be inaccurate or incomplete or cannot be verified, the consumer reporting agency shall promptly delete that item of information from the consumer's file or modify that item of information, as appropriate, based on the results of the reinvestigation.

(B) Requirements relating to reinsertion of previously deleted material.

(i) Certification of accuracy of information. If any information is deleted from a consumer's file pursuant to subparagraph (A), the information may not be reinserted in the file by the consumer reporting agency unless the person who furnishes the information certifies that the information is complete and accurate.

(ii) Notice to consumer. If any information that has been deleted from a consumer's file pursuant to subparagraph (A) is reinserted in the file, the consumer reporting agency shall notify the consumer of the reinsertion in writing not later than 5 business days after the reinsertion or, if authorized by the consumer for that purpose, by any other means available to the agency.

(iii) Additional information. As part of, or in addition to, the notice under clause (ii), a consumer reporting agency shall provide to a consumer in writing not later than 5 business days after the date of the reinsertion

(I) a statement that the disputed information has been reinserted;

(II) the business name and address of any furnisher of information contacted and the telephone number of such furnisher, if reasonably available, or of any furnisher of information that contacted the consumer reporting agency, in connection with the reinsertion of such information; and

(III) a notice that the consumer has the right to add a statement to the consumer's file disputing the accuracy or completeness of the disputed information.

(C) Procedures to prevent reappearance. A consumer reporting agency shall maintain reasonable procedures designed to prevent the reappearance in a consumer's file, and in consumer reports on the consumer, of information that is deleted pursuant to this paragraph (other than information that is reinserted in accordance with subparagraph (B)(i)).

(D) Automated reinvestigation system. Any consumer reporting agency that compiles and maintains files on consumers on a nationwide basis shall implement an automated system through which furnishers of information to that consumer reporting agency may report the results of a reinvestigation that finds incomplete or inaccurate information in a consumer's file to other such consumer reporting agencies.

(6) Notice of results of reinvestigation.

(A) In general. A consumer reporting agency shall provide written notice to a consumer of the results of a reinvestigation under this subsection not later than 5 business days after the completion of the reinvestigation, by mail or, if authorized by the consumer for that purpose, by other means available to the agency.

(B) Contents. As part of, or in addition to, the notice under subparagraph (A), a consumer reporting agency shall provide to a consumer in writing before the expiration of the 5-day period referred to in subparagraph (A)

(i) a statement that the reinvestigation is completed;

(ii) a consumer report that is based upon the consumer's file as that file is revised as a result of the reinvestigation;

(iii) a notice that, if requested by the consumer, a description of the procedure used to determine the accuracy and completeness of the information shall be provided to the consumer by the agency, including the business name and address of any furnisher of information contacted in connection with such information and the telephone number of such furnisher, if reasonably available;

(iv) a notice that the consumer has the right to add a statement to the consumer's file disputing the accuracy or completeness of the information; and

(v) a notice that the consumer has the right to request under subsection (d) that the consumer reporting agency furnish notifications under that subsection.

(7) Description of reinvestigation procedure. A consumer reporting agency shall provide to a consumer a description referred to in paragraph (6)(B)(iii) by not later than 15 days after receiving a request from the consumer for that description.

(8) Expedited dispute resolution. If a dispute regarding an item of information in a consumer's file at a consumer reporting agency is resolved in accordance with paragraph (5)(A) by the deletion of the disputed information by not later than 3 business days after the date on which the agency receives notice of the dispute from the consumer in accordance with paragraph (1)(A), then the agency shall not be required

to comply with paragraphs (2), (6), and (7) with respect to that dispute if the agency

(A) provides prompt notice of the deletion to the consumer by telephone;

(B) includes in that notice, or in a written notice that accompanies a confirmation and consumer report provided in accordance with subparagraph (C), a statement of the consumer's right to request under subsection (d) that the agency furnish notifications under that subsection; and

(C) provides written confirmation of the deletion and a copy of a consumer report on the consumer that is based on the consumer's file after the deletion, not later than 5 business days after making the deletion.

(b) Statement of dispute. If the reinvestigation does not resolve the dispute, the consumer may file a brief statement setting forth the nature of the dispute. The consumer reporting agency may limit such statements to not more than one hundred words if it provides the consumer with assistance in writing a clear summary of the dispute.

(c) Notification of consumer dispute in subsequent consumer reports. Whenever a statement of a dispute is filed, unless there is reasonable grounds to believe that it is frivolous or irrelevant, the consumer reporting agency shall, in any subsequent consumer report containing the information in question, clearly note that it is disputed by the consumer and provide either the consumer's statement or a clear and accurate codification or summary thereof.

(d) Notification of deletion of disputed information. Following any deletion of information which is found to be inaccurate or whose accuracy can no longer be verified or any notation as to disputed information, the consumer reporting agency shall, at the request of the consumer, furnish notification that the item has been deleted or the statement, codification or summary pursuant to subsection (b) or (c) of this section to any person specifically designated by the consumer who has within two years prior thereto received a consumer report for employment purposes, or within six months prior thereto received a consumer report for any other purpose, which contained the deleted or disputed information.

§ 612. Charges for certain disclosures [15 U.S.C. § 1681j]

(a) Reasonable charges allowed for certain disclosures.

(1) In general. Except as provided in subsections (b), (c), and (d), a consumer reporting agency may impose a reasonable charge on a consumer

(A) for making a disclosure to the consumer pursuant to section 609 [§

1681g], which charge

(i) shall not exceed $8; and

(ii) shall be indicated to the consumer before making the disclosure; and

(B) for furnishing, pursuant to 611(d) [§ 1681i], following a reinvestigation under section 611(a) [§ 1681i], a statement, codification, or summary to a person designated by the consumer under that section after the 30-day period beginning on the date of notification of the consumer under paragraph (6) or (8) of section 611(a) [§ 1681i] with respect to the reinvestigation, which charge

(i) shall not exceed the charge that the agency would impose on each designated recipient for a consumer report; and

(ii) shall be indicated to the consumer before furnishing such information.

(2) Modification of amount. The Federal Trade Commission shall increase the amount referred to in paragraph (1)(A)(I) on January 1 of each year, based proportionally on changes in the Consumer Price Index, with fractional changes rounded to the nearest fifty cents.

(b) Free disclosure after adverse notice to consumer. Each consumer reporting agency that maintains a file on a consumer shall make all disclosures pursuant to section 609 [§ 1681g] without charge to the consumer if, not later than 60 days after receipt by such consumer of a notification pursuant to section 615 [§ 1681m], or of a notification from

a debt collection agency affiliated with that consumer reporting agency stating that the consumer's credit rating may be or has been adversely affected, the consumer makes a request under section 609 [§ 1681g].

(c) Free disclosure under certain other circumstances. Upon the request of the consumer, a consumer reporting agency shall make all disclosures pursuant to section 609 [§ 1681g] once during any 12-month period without charge to that consumer if the consumer certifies in writing that the consumer

(1) is unemployed and intends to apply for employment in the 60-day period beginning on the date on which the certification is made;

(2) is a recipient of public welfare assistance; or

(3) has reason to believe that the file on the consumer at the agency contains inaccurate information due to fraud.

(d) Other charges prohibited. A consumer reporting agency shall not impose any charge on a consumer for providing any notification required by this title or making any disclosure required by this title, except as authorized by subsection (a).

§ 613. Public record information for employment purposes [15 U.S.C. §

1681k]

(a) In general. A consumer reporting agency which furnishes a consumer report for employment purposes and which for that purpose compiles and reports items of information on consumers which are matters of public record and are likely to have an adverse effect upon a consumer's ability to obtain employment shall

(1) at the time such public record information is reported to the user of such consumer report, notify the consumer of the fact that public record information is being reported by the consumer reporting agency, together with the name and address of the person to whom such information is being reported; or

(2) maintain strict procedures designed to insure that whenever public record information which is likely to have an adverse effect on a consumer's ability to obtain employment is reported it is complete and up to date. For purposes of this paragraph, items of public record relating to arrests, indictments, convictions, suits, tax liens, and outstanding judgments shall be considered up to date if the current public record status of the item at the time of the report is reported.

(b) Exemption for national security investigations. Subsection (a) does not apply in the case of an agency or department of the United States Government that seeks to obtain and use a consumer report for employment purposes, if the head of the agency or department makes a written finding as prescribed under section 604(b)(4)(A).

§ 614. Restrictions on investigative consumer reports [15 U.S.C. § 1681l]

Whenever a consumer reporting agency prepares an investigative consumer report, no adverse information in the consumer report (other than information which is a matter of public record) may be included in a subsequent consumer report unless such adverse information has been verified in the process of making such subsequent consumer report, or the adverse information was received within the three-month period preceding the date the subsequent report is furnished.

§ 615. Requirements on users of consumer reports [15 U.S.C. § 1681m]

(a) Duties of users taking adverse actions on the basis of information contained in consumer reports. If any person takes any adverse action with respect to any consumer that is based in whole or in part on any information contained in a consumer report, the person shall

(1) provide oral, written, or electronic notice of the adverse action to the consumer;

(2) provide to the consumer orally, in writing, or electronically

(A) the name, address, and telephone number of the consumer reporting agency (including a toll-free telephone number established by the agency if the agency compiles and maintains files on consumers on a nationwide basis) that furnished the report to the person; and

(B) a statement that the consumer reporting agency did not make the decision to take the adverse action and is unable to provide the consumer the specific reasons why the adverse action was taken; and

(3) provide to the consumer an oral, written, or electronic notice of the consumer's right

(A) to obtain, under section 612 [§ 1681j], a free copy of a consumer report on the consumer from the consumer reporting agency referred to in paragraph (2), which notice shall include an indication of the 60-day period under that section for obtaining such a copy; and

(B) to dispute, under section 611 [§ 1681i], with a consumer reporting agency the accuracy or completeness of any information in a consumer report furnished by the agency.

(b) Adverse action based on information obtained from third parties other than consumer reporting agencies.

(1) In general. Whenever credit for personal, family, or household purposes involving a consumer is denied or the charge for such credit is increased either wholly or partly because of information obtained from a person other than a consumer reporting agency bearing upon the consumer's credit worthiness, credit standing, credit capacity, character, general reputation, personal characteristics, or mode of living, the user of such information shall, within a reasonable period of time, upon the consumer's written request for the reasons for such adverse action received within sixty days after learning of such adverse action, disclose the nature of the information to the consumer. The user of such information shall clearly and accurately disclose to the consumer his right to make such written request at the time such adverse action is communicated to the consumer.

(2) Duties of person taking certain actions based on information provided by affiliate.

(A) Duties, generally. If a person takes an action described in subparagraph (B) with respect to a consumer, based in whole or in part on information described in subparagraph (C), the person shall

(i) notify the consumer of the action, including a statement that the consumer may obtain the information in accordance with clause (ii); and

(ii) upon a written request from the consumer received within 60 days after transmittal of the notice required by clause (I), disclose to the consumer the nature of the information upon which the action is based by not later than 30 days after receipt of the request.

(B) Action described. An action referred to in subparagraph (A) is an adverse action described in section 603(k)(1)(A) [§ 1681a], taken in connection with a transaction initiated by the consumer, or any adverse action described in clause (i) or (ii) of section 603(k)(1)(B) [§ 1681a].

(C) Information described. Information referred to in subparagraph (A)

(i) except as provided in clause (ii), is information that

(I) is furnished to the person taking the action by a person related by common ownership or affiliated by common corporate control to the person taking the action; and

(II) bears on the credit worthiness, credit standing, credit capacity, character, general reputation, personal characteristics, or mode of living of the consumer; and

(ii) does not include

(I) information solely as to transactions or experiences between the consumer and the person furnishing the information; or

(II) information in a consumer report.

(c) Reasonable procedures to assure compliance. No person shall be held liable for any violation of this section if he shows by a preponderance of the evidence that at the time of the alleged violation he maintained reasonable procedures to assure compliance with the provisions of this section.

(d) Duties of users making written credit or insurance solicitations on the basis of information contained in consumer files.

(1) In general. Any person who uses a consumer report on any consumer in connection with any credit or insurance transaction that is not initiated by the consumer, that is provided to that person under section 604(c)(1)(B) [§ 1681b], shall provide with each written solicitation made to the consumer regarding the transaction a clear and conspicuous statement that

(A) information contained in the consumer's consumer report was used in connection with the transaction;

(B) the consumer received the offer of credit or insurance because the consumer satisfied the criteria for credit worthiness or insurability under which the consumer was selected for the offer;

(C) if applicable, the credit or insurance may not be extended if, after the consumer responds to the offer, the consumer does not meet the criteria used to select the consumer for the offer or any applicable criteria bearing on credit worthiness or insurability or does not furnish any required collateral;

(D) the consumer has a right to prohibit information contained in the consumer's file with any consumer reporting agency from being used in connection with any credit or insurance transaction that is not initiated by the consumer; and

(E) the consumer may exercise the right referred to in subparagraph (D) by notifying a notification system established under section 604(e) [§ 1681b].

(2) Disclosure of address and telephone number. A statement under paragraph (1) shall include the address and toll-free telephone number of the appropriate notification system established under section 604(e) [§ 1681b].

(3) Maintaining criteria on file. A person who makes an offer of credit or insurance to a consumer under a credit or insurance transaction described in paragraph (1) shall maintain on file the criteria used to select the consumer to receive the offer, all criteria bearing on credit worthiness or insurability, as applicable, that are the basis for determining whether or not to extend credit or insurance pursuant to the offer, and any requirement for the furnishing of collateral as a condition of the extension of credit or insurance, until the expiration of the 3-year period beginning on the date on which the offer is made to the consumer.

(4) Authority of federal agencies regarding unfair or deceptive acts or practices not affected. This section is not intended to affect the authority of any Federal or State agency to enforce a prohibition against unfair or deceptive acts or practices, including the making of false or misleading statements in connection with a credit or insurance transaction that is not initiated by the consumer.

§ 616. Civil liability for willful noncompliance [15 U.S.C. § 1681n]

(a) In general. Any person who willfully fails to comply with any requirement imposed under this title with respect to any consumer is liable to that consumer in an amount equal to the sum of

(1) (A) any actual damages sustained by the consumer as a result of the failure or damages of not less than $100 and not more than $1,000; or

(B) in the case of liability of a natural person for obtaining a consumer report under false pretenses or knowingly without a permissible purpose, actual damages sustained by the consumer as a result of the failure or $1,000, whichever is greater;

(2) such amount of punitive damages as the court may allow; and

(3) in the case of any successful action to enforce any liability under this section, the costs of the action together with reasonable attorney's fees as determined by the court.

(b) Civil liability for knowing noncompliance. Any person who obtains a consumer report from a consumer reporting agency under false pretenses or knowingly without a permissible purpose shall be liable to the consumer reporting agency for actual damages sustained by the consumer reporting agency or $1,000, whichever is greater.

(c) Attorney's fees. Upon a finding by the court that an unsuccessful pleading, motion, or other paper filed in connection with an action under this section was filed in bad faith or for purposes of harassment, the court shall award to the prevailing party attorney's fees reasonable in relation to the work expended in responding to the pleading, motion, or other paper.

§ 617. Civil liability for negligent noncompliance [15 U.S.C. § 1681o]

(a) In general. Any person who is negligent in failing to comply with any requirement imposed under this title with respect to any consumer is liable to that consumer in an amount equal to the sum of

(1) any actual damages sustained by the consumer as a result of the failure;

(2) in the case of any successful action to enforce any liability under this section, the costs of the action together with reasonable attorney's fees as determined by the court.

(b) Attorney's fees. On a finding by the court that an unsuccessful pleading, motion, or other paper filed in connection with an action under this section was filed in bad faith or for purposes of harassment, the court shall award to the prevailing party attorney's fees reasonable in relation to the work expended in responding to the pleading, motion, or other paper.

§ 618. Jurisdiction of courts; limitation of actions [15 U.S.C. § 1681p]

An action to enforce any liability created under this title may be brought in any appropriate United States district court without regard to the amount in controversy, or in any other court of competent jurisdiction, within two years from the date on which the liability arises, except that where a defendant has materially and willfully misrepresented any information required under this title to be disclosed to an individual and the information so misrepresented is material to the establishment of the defendant's liability to that individual under this title, the action may be brought at any time within two years after discovery by the individual of the misrepresentation.

§ 619. Obtaining information under false pretenses [15 U.S.C. § 1681q]

Any person who knowingly and willfully obtains information on a consumer from a consumer reporting agency under false pretenses shall be fined under title 18, United States Code, imprisoned for not more than 2 years, or both.

§ 620. Unauthorized disclosures by officers or employees [15 U.S.C. § 1681r]

Any officer or employee of a consumer reporting agency who knowingly and willfully provides information concerning an individual from the agency's files to a person not authorized to receive that information shall be fined under title 18, United States Code, imprisoned for not more than 2 years, or both.

§ 621. Administrative enforcement [15 U.S.C. § 1681s]

(a) (1) Enforcement by Federal Trade Commission. Compliance with the requirements imposed under this title shall be enforced under the Federal Trade Commission Act [15 U.S.C. §§ 41 et seq.] by the Federal Trade Commission with respect to consumer reporting agencies and all other persons subject thereto, except to the extent that enforcement of the requirements imposed under this title is specifically committed to some other government agency under subsection (b) hereof. For the purpose of the exercise by the Federal Trade Commission of its functions and powers under the Federal Trade Commission Act, a violation of any requirement or prohibition imposed under this title shall constitute an unfair or deceptive act or practice in commerce in violation of section 5(a) of the Federal Trade Commission Act [15 U.S.C. § 45(a)] and shall be subject to enforcement by the Federal Trade Commission under section 5(b) thereof [15 U.S.C. § 45(b)] with respect to any consumer reporting agency or person subject to enforcement by the Federal Trade Commission pursuant to this subsection, irrespective of whether that person is engaged in commerce or meets any other jurisdictional tests in the Federal Trade Commission Act. The Federal Trade Commission shall have such procedural, investigative, and enforcement powers, including the power to issue procedural rules in enforcing compliance with the requirements imposed under this title and to require the filing of reports, the production of documents, and the appearance of witnesses as though the applicable terms and conditions of the Federal Trade Commission Act were part of this title. Any person violating any of the provisions of this title shall be subject to the penalties and entitled to the privileges and immunities provided in the Federal Trade Commission Act as though the applicable terms and provisions thereof were part of this title.

2) (A) In the event of a knowing violation, which constitutes a pattern or practice of violations of this title, the Commission may commence a civil action to recover a civil penalty in a district court of the United States against any person that violates this title. In such action, such person shall be liable for a civil penalty of not more than $2,500 per violation.

(B) In determining the amount of a civil penalty under subparagraph (A), the court shall take into account the degree of culpability, any history of prior such conduct, ability to pay, effect on ability to continue to do business, and such other matters as justice may require.

(3) Notwithstanding paragraph (2), a court may not impose any civil penalty on a person for a violation of section 623(a)(1) [§ 1681s-2] unless the person has been enjoined from committing the violation, or ordered not to commit the violation, in an action or proceeding brought by or on behalf of the Federal Trade Commission, and has violated the injunction or order, and the court may not impose any civil penalty for any violation occurring before the date of the violation of the injunction or order.

(4) Neither the Commission nor any other agency referred to in subsection (b) may prescribe trade regulation rules or other regulations with respect to this title.

(b) Enforcement by other agencies. Compliance with the requirements imposed under this title with respect to consumer reporting agencies, persons who use consumer reports from such agencies, persons who furnish information to such agencies, and users of information that are subject to subsection (d) of section 615 [§ 1681m] shall be enforced under

(1) section 8 of the Federal Deposit Insurance Act [12 U.S.C. § 1818], in the case of

(A) national banks, and Federal branches and Federal agencies of foreign banks, by the Office of the Comptroller of the Currency;

(B) member banks of the Federal Reserve System (other than national banks), branches and agencies of foreign banks (other than Federal branches, Federal agencies, and insured State branches of foreign banks), commercial lending companies owned or controlled by foreign banks, and organizations operating under section 25 or 25(a) [25A] of the Federal Reserve Act [12 U.S.C. §§ 601 et seq., §§ 611 et seq], by the Board of Governors of the Federal Reserve System; and

(C) banks insured by the Federal Deposit Insurance Corporation (other than members of the Federal Reserve System) and insured State branches of foreign banks, by the Board of Directors of the Federal Deposit Insurance Corporation;

(2) section 8 of the Federal Deposit Insurance Act [12 U.S.C. § 1818], by the Director of the Office of Thrift Supervision, in the case of a savings association the deposits of which are insured by the Federal Deposit Insurance Corporation;

(3) the Federal Credit Union Act [12 U.S.C. §§ 1751 et seq.], by the Administrator of the National Credit Union Administration [National Credit Union Administration Board] with respect to any Federal credit union;

(4) subtitle IV of title 49 [49 U.S.C. §§ 10101 et seq.], by the Secretary of Transportation, with respect to all carriers subject to the jurisdiction of the Surface Transportation Board;

(5) the Federal Aviation Act of 1958 [49 U.S.C. Appx §§ 1301 et seq.], by the Secretary of Transportation with respect to any air carrier or foreign air carrier subject to that Act [49 U.S.C. Appx §§ 1301 et seq.]; and

(6) the Packers and Stockyards Act, 1921 [7 U.S.C. §§ 181 et seq.] (except as provided in section 406 of that Act [7 U.S.C. §§ 226 and 227]), by the Secretary of Agriculture with respect to any activities subject to that Act.

The terms used in paragraph (1) that are not defined in this title or otherwise defined in section 3(s) of the Federal Deposit Insurance Act (12 U.S.C. § 1813(s)) shall have the meaning given to them in section 1(b) of the International Banking Act of 1978 (12 U.S.C. § 3101).

(c) State action for violations.

(1) Authority of states. In addition to such other remedies as are provided under State law, if the chief law enforcement officer of a State, or an official or agency designated by a State, has reason to believe that any person has violated or is violating this title, the State

(A) may bring an action to enjoin such violation in any appropriate United States district court or in any other court of competent jurisdiction;

(B) subject to paragraph (5), may bring an action on behalf of the residents of the State to recover

(i) damages for which the person is liable to such residents under sections 616 and 617 [§§ 1681n and 1681o] as a result of the violation;

(ii) in the case of a violation of section 623(a) [§ 1681s-2], damages for which the person would, but for section 623(c) [§ 1681s-2], be liable to such residents as a result of the violation; or

(iii) damages of not more than $1,000 for each willful or negligent violation; and

(C) in the case of any successful action under subparagraph (A) or (B), shall be awarded the costs of the action and reasonable attorney fees as determined by the court.

(2) Rights of federal regulators. The State shall serve prior written notice of any action under paragraph (1) upon the Federal Trade Commission or the appropriate Federal regulator determined under subsection (b) and provide the Commission or appropriate Federal regulator with a copy of its complaint, except in any case in which such prior notice is not feasible, in which case the State shall serve such notice immediately upon instituting such action. The Federal Trade Commission or appropriate Federal regulator shall have the right

(A) to intervene in the action;

(B) upon so intervening, to be heard on all matters arising therein;

(C) to remove the action to the appropriate United States district court; and

(D) to file petitions for appeal.

(3) Investigatory powers. For purposes of bringing any action under this subsection, nothing in this subsection shall prevent the chief law enforcement officer, or an official or agency designated by a State, from exercising the powers conferred on the chief law enforcement officer or such official by the laws of such State to conduct investigations or to administer oaths or affirmations or to compel the attendance of witnesses or the production of documentary and other evidence.

(4) Limitation on state action while federal action pending. If the Federal Trade Commission or the appropriate Federal regulator has instituted a civil action or an administrative action under section 8 of the Federal Deposit Insurance Act for a violation of this title, no State may, during the pendency of such action, bring an action under this section against any defendant named in the complaint of the Commission or the appropriate Federal regulator for any violation of this title that is alleged in that complaint.

(5) Limitations on state actions for violation of section 623(a)(1) [§ 1681s-2].

(A) Violation of injunction required. A State may not bring an action against a person under paragraph (1)(B) for a violation of section

623(a)(1) [§ 1681s-2], unless

(i) the person has been enjoined from committing the violation, in an action brought by the State under paragraph (1)(A); and

(ii) the person has violated the injunction.

(B) Limitation on damages recoverable. In an action against a person under paragraph (1)(B) for a violation of section 623(a)(1) [§ 1681s-2], a State may not recover any damages incurred before the date of the violation of an injunction on which the action is based.

(d) Enforcement under other authority. For the purpose of the exercise by any agency referred to in subsection (b) of this section of its powers under any Act referred to in that subsection, a violation of any requirement imposed under this title shall be deemed to be a violation of a requirement imposed under that Act. In addition to its powers under any provision of law specifically referred to in subsection (b) of this section, each of the agencies referred to in that subsection may exercise, for the purpose of enforcing compliance with any requirement imposed under this title any other authority conferred on it by law. Notwithstanding the preceding, no agency referred to in subsection (b) may conduct an examination of a bank, savings association, or credit union regarding compliance with the provisions of this title, except in response to a complaint (or if the agency otherwise has knowledge) that the bank, savings association, or credit union has violated a provision of this title, in which case, the agency may conduct an examination as necessary to investigate the complaint. If an agency determines during an investigation in response to a complaint that a violation of this title has occurred, the agency may, during its next 2 regularly scheduled examinations of the bank, savings association, or credit union, examine for compliance with this title.

(e) Interpretive authority. The Board of Governors of the Federal Reserve System may issue interpretations of any provision of this title as such provision may apply to any persons identified under paragraph (1), (2), and (3) of subsection (b), or to the holding companies and affiliates of such persons, in consultation with Federal agencies identified in

paragraphs (1), (2), and (3) of subsection (b).

§ 622. Information on overdue child support obligations [15 U.S.C. § 1681s-1]

Notwithstanding any other provision of this title, a consumer reporting agency shall include in any consumer report furnished by the agency in accordance with section 604 [§ 1681b] of this title, any information on the failure of the consumer to pay overdue support which

(1) is provided

(A) to the consumer reporting agency by a State or local child support enforcement agency; or

(B) to the consumer reporting agency and verified by any local, State, or Federal government agency; and

(2) antedates the report by 7 years or less.

§ 623. Responsibilities of furnishers of information to consumer reporting agencies [15 U.S.C. § 1681s-2]

(a) Duty of furnishers of information to provide accurate information.

(1) Prohibition.

(A) Reporting information with actual knowledge of errors. A person shall not furnish any information relating to a consumer to any consumer reporting agency if the person knows or consciously avoids knowing that the information is inaccurate.

(B) Reporting information after notice and confirmation of errors. A person shall not furnish information relating to a consumer to any consumer reporting agency if

(i) the person has been notified by the consumer, at the address specified by the person for such notices, that specific information is inaccurate; and

(ii) the information is, in fact, inaccurate.

(C) No address requirement. A person who clearly and conspicuously specifies to the consumer an address for notices referred to in subparagraph (B) shall not be subject to subparagraph (A); however, nothing in subparagraph (B) shall require a person to specify such an address.

(2) Duty to correct and update information. A person who

(A) regularly and in the ordinary course of business furnishes information to one or more consumer reporting agencies about the person's transactions or experiences with any consumer; and

(B) has furnished to a consumer reporting agency information that the person determines is not complete or accurate,

shall promptly notify the consumer reporting agency of that determination and provide to the agency any corrections to that information, or any additional information, that is necessary to make the information provided by the person to the agency complete and accurate, and shall not thereafter furnish to the agency any of the information that remains not complete or accurate.

(3) Duty to provide notice of dispute. If the completeness or accuracy of any information furnished by any person to any consumer reporting agency is disputed to such person by a consumer, the person may not furnish the information to any consumer reporting agency without notice that such information is disputed by the consumer.

(4) Duty to provide notice of closed accounts. A person who regularly and in the ordinary course of business furnishes information to a consumer reporting agency regarding a consumer who has a credit account with that person shall notify the agency of the voluntary closure of the account by the consumer, in information regularly furnished for the period in which the account is closed.

(5) Duty to provide notice of delinquency of accounts. A person who furnishes information to a consumer reporting agency regarding a delinquent account being placed for collection, charged to profit or loss, or subjected to any similar action shall, not later than 90 days after furnishing the information, notify the agency of the month and year of the commencement of the delinquency that immediately preceded the action.

(b) Duties of furnishers of information upon notice of dispute.

(1) In general. After receiving notice pursuant to section 611(a)(2) [§ 1681i] of a dispute with regard to the completeness or accuracy of any information provided by a person to a consumer reporting agency, the person shall

(A) conduct an investigation with respect to the disputed information;

(B) review all relevant information provided by the consumer reporting agency pursuant to section 611(a)(2) [§ 1681i];

(C) report the results of the investigation to the consumer reporting agency; and

(D) if the investigation finds that the information is incomplete or inaccurate, report those results to all other consumer reporting agencies to which the person furnished the information and that compile and maintain files on consumers on a nationwide basis.

(2) Deadline. A person shall complete all investigations, reviews, and reports required under paragraph (1) regarding information provided by the person to a consumer reporting agency, before the expiration of the period under section 611(a)(1) [§ 1681i] within which the consumer reporting agency is required to complete actions required by that section regarding that information.

(c) Limitation on liability. Sections 616 and 617 [§§ 1681n and 1681o] do not apply to any failure to comply with subsection (a), except as provided in section 621(c)(1)(B) [§ 1681s].

(d) Limitation on enforcement. Subsection (a) shall be enforced exclusively under section 621 [§ 1681s] by the Federal agencies and officials and the State officials identified in that section.

§ 624. Relation to State laws [15 U.S.C. § 1681t]

(a) In general. Except as provided in subsections (b) and (c), this title does not annul, alter, affect, or exempt any person subject to the provisions of this title from complying with the laws of any State with respect to the collection, distribution, or use of any information on consumers, except to the extent that those laws are inconsistent with any provision of this title, and then only to the extent of the inconsistency.

(b) General exceptions. No requirement or prohibition may be imposed under the laws of any State

(1) with respect to any subject matter regulated under

(A) subsection (c) or (e) of section 604 [§ 1681b], relating to the prescreening of consumer reports;

(B) section 611 [§ 1681i], relating to the time by which a consumer reporting agency must take any action, including the provision of notification to a consumer or other person, in any procedure related to the disputed accuracy of information in a consumer's file, except that this subparagraph shall not apply to any State law in effect on the date of enactment of the Consumer Credit Reporting Reform Act of 1996;

(C) subsections (a) and (b) of section 615 [§ 1681m], relating to the duties of a person who takes any adverse action with respect to a consumer;

(D) section 615(d) [§ 1681m], relating to the duties of persons who use a consumer report of a consumer in connection with any credit or insurance transaction that is not initiated by the consumer and that consists of a firm offer of credit or insurance;

(E) section 605 [§ 1681c], relating to information contained in consumer reports, except that this subparagraph shall not apply to any State law in effect on the date of enactment of the Consumer Credit Reporting Reform Act of 1996; or

(F) section 623 [§ 1681s-2], relating to the responsibilities of persons who furnish information to consumer reporting agencies, except that this paragraph shall not apply

(i) with respect to section 54A(a) of chapter 93 of the Massachusetts Annotated Laws (as in effect on the date of enactment of the Consumer Credit Reporting Reform Act of 1996); or

(ii) with respect to section 1785.25(a) of the California Civil Code (as in effect on the date of enactment of the Consumer Credit Reporting Reform Act of 1996);

(2) with respect to the exchange of information among persons affiliated by common ownership or common corporate control, except that this paragraph shall not apply with respect to subsection (a) or (c)(1) of section 2480e of title 9, Vermont Statutes Annotated (as in effect on the date of enactment of the Consumer Credit Reporting Reform Act of 1996); or

(3) with respect to the form and content of any disclosure required to be made under section 609(c) [§ 1681g].

(c) Definition of firm offer of credit or insurance. Notwithstanding any definition of the term "firm offer of credit or insurance" (or any equivalent term) under the laws of any State, the definition of that term contained in section 603(l) [§ 1681a] shall be construed to apply in the enforcement and interpretation of the laws of any State governing consumer reports.

(d) Limitations. Subsections (b) and (c)

(1) do not affect any settlement, agreement, or consent judgment between any State Attorney General and any consumer reporting agency in effect on the date of enactment of the Consumer Credit Reporting Reform Act of 1996; and

(2) do not apply to any provision of State law (including any provision of a State constitution) that

(A) is enacted after January 1, 2004;

(B) states explicitly that the provision is intended to supplement this title; and

(C) gives greater protection to consumers than is provided under this title.

§ 625. Disclosures to FBI for counterintelligence purposes [15 U.S.C. § 1681u]

(a) Identity of financial institutions. Notwithstanding section 604 [§ 1681b] or any other provision of this title, a consumer reporting agency shall furnish to the Federal Bureau of Investigation the names and addresses of all financial institutions (as that term is defined in section 1101 of the Right to Financial Privacy Act of 1978 [12 U.S.C. § 3401]) at which a consumer maintains or has maintained an account, to the extent that information is in the files of the agency, when presented with a written request for that information, signed by the Director of the Federal Bureau of Investigation, or the Director's designee, which certifies compliance with this section. The Director or the Director's designee may make such a certification only if the Director or the Director's designee has determined in writing that

(1) such information is necessary for the conduct of an authorized foreign counterintelligence investigation; and

(2) there are specific and articulable facts giving reason to believe that the consumer

(A) is a foreign power (as defined in section 101 of the Foreign Intelligence Surveillance Act of 1978 [50 U.S.C. § 1801]) or a person who is not a United States person (as defined in such section 101) and is an official of a foreign power; or

(B) is an agent of a foreign power and is engaging or has engaged in an act of international terrorism (as that term is defined in section 101(c) of the Foreign Intelligence Surveillance Act of 1978 [50 U.S.C. § 1801(c)]) or clandestine intelligence activities that involve or may involve a violation of criminal statutes of the United States.

(b) Identifying information. Notwithstanding the provisions of section 604 [§ 1681b] or any other provision of this title, a consumer reporting agency shall furnish identifying information respecting a consumer, limited to name, address, former addresses, places of employment, or former places of employment, to the Federal Bureau of Investigation when presented with a written request, signed by the Director or the Director's designee, which certifies compliance with this subsection. The Director or the Director's designee may make such a certification only if the Director or the Director's designee has determined in writing that

(1) such information is necessary to the conduct of an authorized counterintelligence investigation; and

(2) there is information giving reason to believe that the consumer has been, or is about to be, in contact with a foreign power or an agent of a foreign power (as defined in section 101 of the Foreign Intelligence Surveillance Act of 1978 [50 U.S.C. § 1801]).

(c) Court order for disclosure of consumer reports. Notwithstanding section 604 [§ 1681b] or any other provision of this title, if requested in writing by the Director of the Federal Bureau of Investigation, or a designee of the Director, a court may issue an order ex parte directing a consumer reporting agency to furnish a consumer report to the Federal Bureau of Investigation, upon a showing in camera that

(1) the consumer report is necessary for the conduct of an authorized foreign counterintelligence investigation; and

(2) there are specific and articulable facts giving reason to believe that the consumer whose consumer report is sought

(A) is an agent of a foreign power, and

(B) is engaging or has engaged in an act of international terrorism (as that term is defined in section 101(c) of the Foreign Intelligence Surveillance Act of 1978 [50 U.S.C. § 1801(c)]) or clandestine intelligence activities that involve or may involve a violation of criminal statutes of the United States.

The terms of an order issued under this subsection shall not disclose that the order is issued for purposes of a counterintelligence investigation.

(d) Confidentiality. No consumer reporting agency or officer, employee, or agent of a consumer reporting agency shall disclose to any person, other than those officers, employees, or agents of a consumer reporting agency necessary to fulfill the requirement to disclose information to the Federal Bureau of Investigation under this section, that the Federal Bureau of Investigation has sought or obtained the identity of financial institutions or a consumer report respecting any consumer under subsection (a), (b), or (c), and no consumer reporting agency or officer, employee, or agent of a consumer reporting agency shall include in any consumer report any information that would indicate that the Federal Bureau of Investigation has sought or obtained such information or a consumer report.

(e) Payment of fees. The Federal Bureau of Investigation shall, subject to the availability of appropriations, pay to the consumer reporting agency assembling or providing report or information in accordance with procedures established under this section a fee for reimbursement for such costs as are reasonably necessary and which have been directly incurred in searching, reproducing, or transporting books, papers, records, or other data required or requested to be produced under this section.

(f) Limit on dissemination. The Federal Bureau of Investigation may not disseminate information obtained pursuant to this section outside of the Federal Bureau of Investigation, except to other Federal agencies as may be necessary for the approval or conduct of a foreign counterintelligence investigation, or, where the information concerns a person subject to the Uniform Code of Military Justice, to appropriate investigative authorities within the military department concerned as may be necessary for the conduct of a joint foreign counterintelligence investigation.

(g) Rules of construction. Nothing in this section shall be construed to prohibit information from being furnished by the Federal Bureau of Investigation pursuant to a subpoena or court order, in connection with a judicial or administrative proceeding to enforce the provisions of this Act. Nothing in this section shall be construed to authorize or permit the withholding of information from the Congress.

(h) Reports to Congress. On a semiannual basis, the Attorney General shall fully inform the Permanent Select Committee on Intelligence and the Committee on Banking, Finance and Urban Affairs of the House of Representatives, and the Select Committee on Intelligence and the Committee on Banking, Housing, and Urban Affairs of the Senate concerning all requests made pursuant to subsections (a), (b), and (c).

(i) Damages. Any agency or department of the United States obtaining or disclosing any consumer reports, records, or information contained therein in violation of this section is liable to the consumer to whom such consumer reports, records, or information relate in an amount equal to the sum of

(1) $100, without regard to the volume of consumer reports, records, or information involved;

(2) any actual damages sustained by the consumer as a result of the disclosure;

(3) if the violation is found to have been willful or intentional, such punitive damages as a court may allow; and

(4) in the case of any successful action to enforce liability under this subsection, the costs of the action, together with reasonable attorney fees, as determined by the court.

(j) Disciplinary actions for violations. If a court determines that any agency or department of the United States has violated any provision of this section and the court finds that the circumstances surrounding the violation raise questions of whether or not an officer or employee of the agency or department acted willfully or intentionally with respect to the violation, the agency or department shall promptly initiate a proceeding to determine whether or not disciplinary action is warranted against the officer or employee who was responsible for the violation.

(k) Good-faith exception. Notwithstanding any other provision of this title, any consumer reporting agency or agent or employee thereof making disclosure of consumer reports or identifying information pursuant to this subsection in good-faith reliance upon a certification of the Federal Bureau of Investigation pursuant to provisions of this section shall not be liable to any person for such disclosure under this title, the constitution of any State, or any law or regulation of any State or any political subdivision of any State.

(l) Limitation of remedies. Notwithstanding any other provision of this title, the remedies and sanctions set forth in this section shall be the only judicial remedies and sanctions for violation of this section.

(m) Injunctive relief. In addition to any other remedy contained in this section, injunctive relief shall be available to require compliance with the procedures of this section. In the event of any successful action under this subsection, costs together with reasonable attorney fees, as determined by the court, may be recovered.

Legislative History

House Reports: No. 91-975 (Comm. on Banking and Currency) and No. 91-1587 (Comm. of Conference)
Senate Reports: No. 91-1139 accompanying S. 3678 (Comm. on Banking and Currency)
Congressional Record, Vol. 116 (1970)

May 25, considered and passed House.
Sept. 18, considered and passed Senate, amended.
Oct. 9, Senate agreed to conference report.
Oct. 13, House agreed to conference report.
Enactment:
Public Law No. 91-508 (October 26, 1970):

Amendments: Public Law Nos.
95-473 (October 17, 1978)
95-598 (November 6, 1978)
98-443 (October 4, 1984)
101-73 (August 9, 1989)
102-242 (December 19, 1991)
102-537 (October 27, 1992)
102-550 (October 28, 1992)
103-325 (September 23, 1994)
104-88 (December 29, 1995)
104-93 (January 6, 1996)
104-193 (August 22, 1996)
104-208 (September 30, 1996)
105-107 (November 20, 1997)
105-347 (November 2, 1998)

1. The reporting periods have been lengthened for certain adverse information pertaining to U.S. Government insured or guaranteed student loans, or pertaining to national direct student loans. See sections 430A(f) and 463(c)(3) of the Higher Education Act of 1965, 20 U.S.C. 1080a(f) and 20 U.S.C. 1087cc(c)(3), respectively.

Credit Repair

Organizations Act

CHAPTER 2—**CREDIT REPAIR ORGANIZATIONS(1)**

SEC. 2451. REGULATION OF CREDIT REPAIR ORGANIZATIONS.

Title IV of the Consumer Credit Protection Act (Public Law 90-321, 82 Stat. 164) is amended to read as follows:

TITLE IV—CREDIT REPAIR ORGANIZATIONS"

SEC. 401. SHORT TITLE.

This title may be cited as the 'Credit Repair Organizations Act'.

SEC. 402. FINDINGS AND PURPOSES.(2)

(a) Findings.—The Congress makes the following findings:

(1) Consumers have a vital interest in establishing and maintaining their credit worthiness and credit standing in order to obtain and use credit. As a result, consumers who have experienced credit problems may seek assistance from credit repair organizations which offer to improve the credit standing of such consumers.
(2) Certain advertising and business practices of some companies engaged in the business of credit repair services have worked a financial hardship upon consumers, particularly those of limited economic means and who are inexperienced in credit matters.
(b) Purposes.—The purposes of this title are—
(1) to ensure that prospective buyers of the services of credit repair organizations are provided with the information necessary to make an informed decision regarding the purchase of such services; and
(2) to protect the public from unfair or deceptive advertising and business practices by credit repair organizations.
SEC. 403. DEFINITIONS.(3)
For purposes of this title, the following definitions apply:
(1) Consumer. — The term 'consumer' means an individual.
(2) Consumer credit transaction. — The term 'consumer credit transaction' means any transaction in which credit is offered or extended to an individual for personal, family, or household purposes.
(3) Credit repair organization. — The term 'credit repair organization'—
(A) means any person who uses any instrumentality of interstate commerce or the mails to sell, provide, or perform (or represent that such person can or will sell, provide, or perform) any service, in return for the payment of money or other valuable consideration, for the express or implied purpose of—
(i) improving any consumer's credit record, credit history, or credit rating; or
(ii) providing advice or assistance to any consumer with regard to any activity or service described in clause (i); and
(B) does not include—
(i) any nonprofit organization which is exempt from taxation under section 501(c)(3) of the Internal Revenue Code of 1986;
(ii) any creditor (as defined in section 103 of the Truth in Lending Act),(4) with respect to any consumer, to the extent the creditor is assisting the consumer to restructure any debt owed by the consumer to the creditor; or
(iii) any depository institution (as that term is defined in section 3 of the Federal Deposit Insurance Act) or any Federal or State credit union (as those terms are defined in section 101 of the Federal Credit Union Act), or any affiliate or subsidiary of such a depository institution or credit union.
(4) Credit.—The term 'credit' has the meaning given to such term in section 103(e) of this Act.(5)

SEC. 404. PROHIBITED PRACTICES.(6)

(a) In General.—No person may—
(1) make any statement, or counsel or advise any consumer to make any statement, which is untrue or misleading (or which, upon the exercise of reasonable care, should be known by the credit repair organization, officer, employee, agent, or other person to be untrue or

]misleading) with respect to any consumer's credit worthiness, credit standing, or credit

capacity to—
(A) any consumer reporting agency (as defined in section 603(f) of this Act);(7) or
(B) any person—
(
i) who has extended credit to the consumer; or
(ii) to whom the consumer has applied or is applying for an extension of credit;
(2) make any statement, or counsel or advise any consumer to make any statement, the intended effect of which is to alter the consumer's identification to prevent the display of the consumer's credit record, history, or rating for the purpose of concealing adverse information that is accurate and not obsolete to—
(A) any consumer reporting agency;
(B) any person—
(i) who has extended credit to the consumer; or
(ii) to whom the consumer has applied or is applying for an extension of credit;
(3) make or use any untrue or misleading representation of the services of the credit repair organization; or
(4) engage, directly or indirectly, in any act, practice, or course of business that constitutes or results in the commission of, or an attempt to commit, a fraud or deception on any person in connection with the offer or sale of the services of the credit repair organization.
(b) Payment in Advance.—No credit repair organization may charge or receive any money or other valuable consideration for the performance of any service which the credit repair organization has agreed to perform for any consumer before such service is fully performed.

SEC. 405. DISCLOSURES.(8)

(a) Disclosure Required.—Any credit repair organization shall provide any consumer with the following written statement before any contract or agreement between the consumer and the credit repair organization is executed:
'Consumer Credit File Rights Under State and Federal Law
You have a right to dispute inaccurate information in your credit report by contacting the credit bureau directly. However, neither you nor any ''credit repair'' company or credit repair organization has the right to have accurate, current, and verifiable information removed from your credit report. The credit bureau must remove accurate, negative information from your report only if it is over 7 years old. Bankruptcy information can be reported for 10 years.
You have a right to obtain a copy of your credit report from a credit bureau. You may be charged a reasonable fee. There is no fee, however, if you have been turned down for credit, employment, insurance, or a rental dwelling because of information in your credit report within the preceding 60 days. The credit bureau must provide someone to help you interpret the information in your credit file. You are entitled to receive a free copy of your credit report if you are unemployed and intend to apply for employment in the next 60 days, if you are a recipient of public welfare assistance, or if you have reason to believe that there is inaccurate information in your credit report due to fraud.
You have a right to sue a credit repair organization that violates the Credit Repair Organization Act. This law prohibits deceptive practices by credit repair organizations.
You have the right to cancel your contract with any credit repair organization for any reason within 3 business days from the date you signed it.

Credit bureaus are required to follow reasonable procedures to ensure that the information they report is accurate. However, mistakes may occur.
You may, on your own, notify a credit bureau in writing that you dispute the accuracy of information in your credit file. The credit bureau must then reinvestigate and modify or remove inaccurate or incomplete information. The credit bureau may not charge any fee

for this service. Any pertinent information and copies of all documents you have concerning an error should be given to the credit bureau.
If the credit bureau's reinvestigation does not resolve the dispute to your satisfaction, you may send a brief statement to the credit bureau, to be kept in your file, explaining why you think the record is inaccurate. The credit bureau must include a summary of your statement about disputed information with any report it issues about you.
The Federal Trade Commission regulates credit bureaus and credit repair organizations. For more information contact:
The Public Reference Branch
Federal Trade Commission
Washington, D.C. 20580'.
(b) Separate Statement Requirement.—The written statement required under this section shall be provided as a document which is separate from any written contract or other agreement between the credit repair organization and the consumer or any other written material provided to the consumer.
(c) Retention of Compliance Records.—
(1) In general.—The credit repair organization shall maintain a copy of the statement signed by the consumer acknowledging receipt of the statement.
(2) Maintenance for 2 years.—The copy of any consumer's statement shall be maintained in the organization's files for 2 years after the date on which the statement is signed by the consumer.

SEC. 406. CREDIT REPAIR ORGANIZATIONS CONTRACTS.(9)

(a) Written Contracts Required.—No services may be provided by any credit repair organization for any consumer—
(1) unless a written and dated contract (for the purchase of such services) which meets the requirements of subsection (b) has been signed by the consumer; or
(2) before the end of the 3-business-day period beginning on the date the contract is signed.
(b) Terms and Conditions of Contract.—No contract referred to in subsection (a) meets the requirements of this subsection unless such contract includes (in writing)—
(1) the terms and conditions of payment, including the total amount of all payments to be made by the consumer to the credit repair organization or to any other person;
(2) a full and detailed description of the services to be performed by the credit repair organization for the consumer, including—
(A) all guarantees of performance; and
(B) an estimate of—
(i) the date by which the performance of the services (to be performed by the credit repair organization or any other person) will be complete; or
(ii) the length of the period necessary to perform such services;
(3) the credit repair organization's name and principal business address; and
(4) a conspicuous statement in bold face type, in immediate proximity to the space reserved for the consumer's signature on the contract, which reads as follows: 'You may cancel this contract without penalty or obligation at any time before midnight of the 3rd

business day after the date on which you signed the contract. See the attached notice of cancellation form for an explanation of this right.'.

SEC. 407. RIGHT TO CANCEL CONTRACT.(10)

(a) In General. — Any consumer may cancel any contract with any credit repair organization without penalty or obligation by notifying the credit repair organization of the consumer's intention to do so at any time before midnight of the 3rd business day which begins after the date on which the contract or agreement between the consumer and the credit repair organization is executed or would, but for this subsection, become enforceable against the parties.

(b) Cancellation Form and Other Information. — Each contract shall be accompanied by a form, in duplicate, which has the heading 'Notice of Cancellation' and contains in bold face type the following statement:

'You may cancel this contract, without any penalty or obligation, at any time before midnight of the 3rd day which begins after the date the contract is signed by you.

To cancel this contract, mail or deliver a signed, dated copy of this cancellation notice, or any other written notice to (name of credit repair organization) at (address of credit repair organization) before midnight on (date)

I hereby cancel this transaction,

(date)

(purchaser's signature).'.

(c) Consumer Copy of Contract Required.—Any consumer who enters into any contract with any credit repair organization shall be given, by the organization—

(1) a copy of the completed contract and the disclosure statement required under section 405; and

(2) a copy of any other document the credit repair organization requires the consumer to sign, at the time the contract or the other document is signed.

SEC. 408. NONCOMPLIANCE WITH THIS TITLE.(11)

(a) Consumer Waivers Invalid.—Any waiver by any consumer of any protection provided by or any right of the consumer under this title—

(1) shall be treated as void; and

(2) may not be enforced by any Federal or State court or any other person.

(b) Attempt To Obtain Waiver.—Any attempt by any person to obtain a waiver from any consumer of any protection provided by or any right of the consumer under this title shall be treated as a violation of this title.

(c) Contracts Not in Compliance.—Any contract for services which does not comply with the applicable provisions of this title—

(1) shall be treated as void; and

(2) may not be enforced by any Federal or State court or any other person.

SEC. 409. CIVIL LIABILITY.(12)

(a) Liability Established.—Any person who fails to comply with any provision of this title with respect to any other person shall be liable to such person in an amount equal to the sum of the amounts determined under each of the following paragraphs:

(1) Actual damages.—The greater of—

(A) the amount of any actual damage sustained by such person as a result of such failure; or

(B) any amount paid by the person to the credit repair organization.

(2) Punitive damages.—

(A) Individual actions.—In the case of any action by an individual, such additional amount as the court may allow.

(B) Class actions.—In the case of a class action, the sum of—
(i) the aggregate of the amount which the court may allow for each named plaintiff; and
(ii) the aggregate of the amount which the court may allow for each other class member, without regard to any minimum individual recovery.

(3) Attorneys' fees.—In the case of any successful action to enforce any liability under paragraph (1) or (2), the costs of the action, together with reasonable attorneys' fees.
(b) Factors to Be Considered in Awarding Punitive Damages.—In determining the amount of any liability of any credit repair organization under subsection (a)(2), the court shall consider, among other relevant factors—
(1) the frequency and persistence of noncompliance by the credit repair organization;
(2) the nature of the noncompliance;
(3) the extent to which such noncompliance was intentional; and
(4) in the case of any class action, the number of consumers adversely affected.

SEC. 410. ADMINISTRATIVE ENFORCEMENT.(13)

(a) In General.—Compliance with the requirements imposed under this title with respect to credit repair organizations shall be enforced under the Federal Trade Commission Act by the Federal Trade Commission.
(b) Violations of This Title Treated as Violations of Federal Trade Commission Act.—
(1) In general. — For the purpose of the exercise by the Federal Trade Commission of the Commission's functions and powers under the Federal Trade Commission Act, any violation of any requirement or prohibition imposed under this title with respect to credit repair organizations shall constitute an unfair or deceptive act or practice in commerce in violation of section 5(a) of the Federal Trade Commission Act.
(2) Enforcement authority under other law. — All functions and powers of the Federal Trade Commission under the Federal Trade Commission Act shall be available to the Commission to enforce compliance with this title by any person subject to enforcement by the Federal Trade Commission pursuant to this subsection, including the power to enforce the provisions of this title in the same manner as if the violation had been a violation of any Federal Trade Commission trade regulation rule, without regard to whether the credit repair organization—
(A) is engaged in commerce; or
(B) meets any other jurisdictional tests in the Federal Trade Commission Act.
(c) State Action for Violations.—
(1) Authority of states. — In addition to such other remedies as are provided under State law, whenever the chief law enforcement officer of a State, or an official or agency designated by a State, has reason to believe that any person has violated or is violating this title, the State—
(A) may bring an action to enjoin such violation;
(B) may bring an action on behalf of its residents to recover damages for which the person is liable to such residents under section 409 as a result of the violation; and
(C) in the case of any successful action under subparagraph (A) or (B), shall be awarded the costs of the action and reasonable attorney fees as determined by the court.
(2) Rights of commission.—
(A) Notice to commission.—The State shall serve prior written notice of any civil action under paragraph (1) upon the Federal Trade Commission and provide the Commission with a copy of its complaint, except in any case where such prior notice is not feasible, in

consumer credit information or other information on consumers for the purpose of furnishing consumer reports to third parties, and which uses any means or facility of interstate commerce for the purpose of preparing or furnishing consumer reports."
8. 15 U.S.C. § 1679c.

9. 15 U.S.C. § 1679d.
10. 15 U.S.C. § 1679e.
11. 15 U.S.C. § 1679f.

12. 15 U.S.C. § 1679g.
13. 15 U.S.C. § 1679h.

14. 15 U.S.C. § 1679i.
15. 15 U.S.C. § 1679j

16. Not codified in United States Code. Cite to Pub. L. 104-28, Div. A, title II, § 2451,

Section 413, 110 Stat. 3009.
17. The statute was signed by the President on September 30, 1996.